THIS BOOK

BELONGS TO

....

....

I can't tell you how grateful I am that you decided to read my book. My most heartfelt thanks that you took time out of your life to choose my work and I hope you find benefit within these pages.

There are so many books available today that offer similar content so that makes it even more humbling that you decided to buying mine.

Tell me what you thought! I am eager to hear your opinion and ideas on what you read as are others who are looking for a good book to buy. Leave a review on Amazon.com so others can benefit from your wisdom!

With much thanks.

Table of Contents

INTRODUCTION

Has your old job-search book passed its sell-by date? Last year's rules don't work today, because Linkedin and other social media have changed everything—and they're still changing. *I Got the Job!* is the only book to cover the latest developments and shows you how to employ them for your own competitive advantage. Nowhere else can you find all this information in one place.

If you want the newest advice and techniques from a career expert on the job search front lines today, I'd like to be your guide. I'm the CEO, a groundbreaking career coaching website, and I also offer career advice weekly on nationally syndicated radio. Based in San Francisco and with clients across America, is a group of expert career coaches and we've seen it all. In this book I'll show you the most common mistakes job seekers make, such as taking jobs they didn't like at companies they didn't fit in to with bosses they didn't get along with. And they did this at salaries that were thousands of dollars and sometimes tens of thousands of dollars less than they should have negotiated for. I'll show you how to avoid these mistakes. I'll also teach you the same methods I use with my clients so you can master your mindset, social media, and out-prepare your competition to get hired in 2013. Before founding I developed my social media and Internet expertise while working in online marketing for fourteen years, most recently as the VP of Marketing at two cutting-edge mobile companies in the San Francisco Bay Area. Previously, I was the Chairman of the Business School at Anglo-American University in Prague where I coached students and alumni on their careers. Today I'm also the Career Affinity Chair of the San Francisco Bay Area alumni association for the Kellogg School of Management at Northwestern University, where I completed my MBA. I completed my BA at the University of Florida, and it was while I lived in

Gainesville that I co-founded Gumby's Pizza, a restaurant chain my partners and I grew to over two hundred employees. My education also includes having completed *Integral Coaching Principles* at New Ventures West, a leading coaching school.

In *this Book!* I guide you through the 8 Steps you need to know to get hired faster—by weeks, if not months. Of course, I can't guarantee this will happen for every single reader, but it will for most using my proven methods. This is the only book on getting hired that begins with "Master Your Mindset" because today it's not enough to do a traditional job search with the old rules. Instead I coach clients on developing their mindfulness through a discovery process that increases their self-awareness and insight into what their true calling is. Additionally, only in this book will you find new methods on how to figure out the ecosystem you thrive best in, how to build your dream team, and how to grow your connections in this social media age. I also explain how you can turn a recruiter into your virtual career agent.

I will guide you through the same proven practices and techniques I use with my clients, which are known by fewer than 10% of professionals. I also explain the social media landscape that matters most in getting hired, including Linkedin, Glassdoor, Facebook, and Twitter. Additionally, I do a deep dive into Linkedin and detail for you the steps you need to take to create a great Linkedin profile that recruiters will respond to. During this "Master Your Social Media" step I walk you through the 4 Steps you should take on Linkedin to get introduced to hiring managers. One executive who was recently in one of my paid Linkedin workshops said he had not received an inbound inquiry from a recruiter in over three years. After completing my workshop he updated his Linkedin profile using the same techniques I detail in Chapter 13. One month later, he was contacted by an executive recruiter via Linkedin for a tremendous Chief Financial Officer opportunity.

Are you ready to turn the page on old, outdated job search efforts and start using specific strategies and methods that are proven to increase your chances of getting hired in this social media age? Do you want to learn how to navigate your job search so you end up in a job you love and at a higher salary? Then turn the page and accelerate your steps to get hired.

Mark Andersen

San Francisco

2013

PROLOGUE: *IT ALL STARTED THE DAY SHE GOT THE JOB.*

Lisa had never felt this before in any of her previous jobs. This was her third job in her career and this sensation was strangely new. She took her first job out of college because she needed to work and start paying off her student loans. She thought she'd enjoy her job a lot more than she did. Lisa couldn't believe she stayed there six years, but it was good experience and the company looked impressive on her resume. She jumped to her second job because it paid a lot more. She was smart, had developed excellent experience, and people naturally liked her. But there was a problem —her new boss was difficult to work for. At first she thought she could work around him, but she found out he was too much of micromanager for that to work. Lisa endured that job for four years until she'd had had enough and decided to find her next job. But this time she didn't want to just jump without thinking this one through or leave for another company just for a big raise. So, she proactively planned her search in order to find the right job at the right company with the right boss. Through her inspired action Lisa found the right job five months later and now here she was in her fourth week in her new job. This was her third job in her career and she realized what those new feelings were: Satisfaction. And happiness. Even joy!

Maybe she shouldn't have been surprised—she worked hard to get here. But after her first two jobs she'd come to believe she could only find fulfillment outside of work. And yet, here she was, loving her new job. Really loving it. She thought she'd like her new boss, not love her, and that turned out to be true. She wasn't going to ever become close friends with her boss, but that was fine. The most important thing to Lisa was that she trusted her new boss. Her boss had her back and was an excellent mentor. And Lisa loved her company culture. She got a raise to take this new job, but not as big of a percentage jump as she did when she took her second jump. But Lisa didn't care about that—this was the first time in her career she wasn't viewing her job as something painful to get up for each morning. Work didn't feel like work anymore. It was…fun! It gave her a sense of mastery, a feeling of calm. And yes, joy.

It all started the day she got the job.

For Lisa this was part of her journey and it's a journey for you and me, too. I intentionally didn't title this book how to get hired "overnight" because it was important for me to not over-promise. A journey takes work. You have to work to take the 8 Steps in this book.

As important as it was for me not to over-promise, it's just as important that I not under-promise.

If you're doing a job search now and you take all 8 Steps in this book you'll almost certainly get hired more quickly as a result. More importantly, you'll increase your likelihood of getting hired for a more fulfilling job. If, in the beginning of your search you're feeling frustrated and anxious, know that most job seekers feel the same way. If ever people need to be positive and send their inner critic on a vacation it's during the trying periods of a job search. Don't be so tough on yourself. You can't take 8 Steps at once, so take them one at a time and honor your progress. You may not feel like you're making progress fast enough, but your small, consistent steps forward will lead to life-changing events over time.

Step One: Master Your Mindset

The cutting-edge techniques you need to maintain a positive mindset – no matter what.

Chapter 1: How to Master Your Mindset

Being a champion has to do with mental toughness more than anything else. There is not much that the top-level athletes do differently from each other, but some win, others don't.

Michael Phelps, American swimmer and most decorated Olympian in history: 18 Gold medals, 22 total medals.

Doing a job search is one of the most vulnerable periods of a person's life. People dread this experience for a variety of valid reasons, but one of the biggest reasons is that they feel like they don't control their job search. As a result, people who have lost their job, people who have decided to leave their current company, and recent college graduates often feel like they're an unanchored ship, drifting uncontrollably at sea, unable to set their direction while being battered by punishing storms. At this critical point when job seekers should be doing their search mindfully, they instead feel a lack of control that hurts their mindset and they lose confidence, become distracted, demoralized, and sometimes even depressed.

The good news is that of the 8 Steps you need to take to get hired, you control or at least greatly influence every single one. Once people realize this fact their old mindset starts swinging from the negative and being distracted back to a purposeful mindset. This mindset shift enables people to focus their attention on getting hired for a meaningful opportunity and it fundamentally changes how they view getting hired as seen below.

Old mindset: Scarcity of jobs: "There aren't many jobs out there."

New mindset: Abundance: "I have multiple opportunities."

Old mindset: Passive, reactive: "Why aren't recruiters contacting me?"

New mindset: Proactive: "I'm building partnerships with 3-4 virtual career agents."

Old mindset: "Social media scares me."

New mindset: "I'm mastering my social media to gain an edge."

Old mindset: "If I don't get the job my preparation was a waste of time."

New mindset: "Preparation drastically increases my chances of getting hired for a job I'll love."

Old mindset: "I don't control my job search."

New mindset: "I control most of my job search and greatly influence the rest."

Old mindset: "I'm being judged during interviews."

New mindset: "The hiring manager and I are having a conversation to mutually determine if I'm a great fit."

Old mindset: "I'm not sure what I want to do next and I'll jump at whatever job comes my way."

New mindset: "I've developed greater self-awareness about what matters to me in my life and career. I'm using this insight to intentionally focus my job search on a few opportunities that will be more rewarding for me."

Old mindset: "My job search is confusing and overwhelming."

New mindset: "I'm taking the 8 Steps and they give me clarity and confidence as to what I have to do to get hired."

Of course there's plenty in getting hired that you don't control. How would you know that your alma mater brings up bad memories for the hiring manager that is interviewing you because his ex-girlfriend (who dumped him) went to your university? You don't control if the company decides to hire an internal candidate. And you don't control if another candidate has 90% of the skill set the company wants and you have 80%. If you focus on your uncontrollables you'll drive yourself crazy with worry, so forget about those areas. Instead, control your controllables. By doing so you'll start moving from being reactive to being proactive in getting hired.

Even after realizing they control the key steps in getting hired, some people still feel stuck. If this is you, don't worry. By creating a metaphor for your old mindset and a metaphor for your new mindset you'll start stepping forward towards getting hired.

YOUR MINDSET METAPHORS

A metaphor is a figure of speech or image that is representative of something else. This figure of speech could be "dream team," "hit a home run," or "climb Mt. Everest." Metaphors aren't meant literally. They're conceptual frameworks that give people a greater form of expression and insight into their lives and they distill entire stories down to one essential word, phrase, or image. Metaphors use a visual image to evoke more profound meaning. For example, here in San Francisco the Golden Gate Bridge is not just a bridge; it's a metaphor for the gateway to possibility, majestic beauty, and human achievement. Two other examples are the Eiffel Tower and the Taj Mahal. In the literal sense you could say one is a tower and the other a palace, but as metaphors for romance and eternal love both have far deeper meaning for billions of people around the world. Songs and books have been written about all three and every year people get engaged at all three locations.

Your Old Metaphor

There are few elements of a job search that cause as much anxiety as the job interview. People typically feel that they're being evaluated, which they are, but this can feel like an interrogation. One person I was coaching, Charlie, described the stressful experience of being drilled question after question by hiring managers who sat there stone faced after every response. He had an upcoming interview that I was coaching him for and it was important to him. After hearing more detail, I offered Charlie a metaphor that I envisioned for him based on his old mindset. I said he was a suspect from a 1940s detective movie, arrested and taken by the police into an interrogation room. The two cops sat him down in a chair that was too low as they stood lording over him, shining a blinding light into his eyes. Under this pressure Charlie started to sweat, squirm in his chair and panic as he looked for the nearest exit.

Charlie laughed in acknowledgement once I finished. He said he'd never thought of it that way, but, yes, that was how he felt. He hated that feeling! He wanted to change it, but he didn't know how to get out of that trapped feeling. Offering a metaphor like this to a client is what James Flaherty, founder of New Ventures West, one of the world's leading coaching schools, calls "compassionate dislodgement." Because it's often difficult for a person to see their own narrative, the goal is to offer the client a current narrative in a compassionate way.

I completed a coaching class at New Ventures West, which is based here in San Francisco. During that training we created an old metaphor and a new metaphor for the person we were coaching and it was very powerful.

Your New Metaphor

Once Charlie had a better understanding of his old mindset through this metaphor, I offered him a new metaphor to suggest a meaningful goal. This new metaphor was based on the outcome he wanted to achieve. As Flaherty explains in his groundbreaking book, *Coaching: Evoking Excellence in Others*, when a new metaphor is offered and it resonates with the client, then they start to focus on new possibilities and new actions in a hopeful, ambitious way. For Charlie, the outcome he wanted was to transform his feeling of anxiety during interviews into a feeling of calm confidence where he could have a conversation about how his creative work would benefit the company. He wanted to feel mastery. At this point we'd spent enough time together for me to know that Charlie was a huge fan of the hit cable show *Mad Men*. I offered to Charlie the new metaphor that he was Don Draper, making his brilliant presentation to Kodak in the episode called "The Wheel." As I expected, Charlie knew the episode.

I told Charlie that if during his next interview he started to feel as if he was being interrogated again, to visualize standing up from his chair so that he was on the same level as the cops. Once he was on their level he could visualize them turning into friendly people from the company he's interviewing at. Then I asked Charlie to visualize turning the light away from his face and towards the wall, just like the projector Don Draper so eloquently used to pitch Kodak. I told Charlie this was no longer an interrogation of him, nor was he going to interrogate the people from the company. They were equals. The focus instead was on Charlie's work, which spoke for itself. He always knew it was excellent, but he was reluctant to own that.

I've offered metaphors before that didn't resonate, but Charlie immediately connected with his new metaphor of him being Don Draper pitching his work to Kodak. Charlie was too modest to say his work was outstanding, but with his new mindset that he was connecting with his inner Don Draper it seemed easier for Charlie to assert himself. Charlie's interview went well, but he didn't get an offer immediately. Instead, they asked him in for another round and he got the offer after that, which he accepted. He described his new feelings in this final interview as a confidence he hadn't had before and a belief in his mastery.

Creating an Anchor to Return to Your Zone

Of course it's not possible to always stay in your "zone" and it wasn't for Charlie either. By zone I mean that state of focused concentration where your performance is elevated. So, we created what is called an "anchor" or a conditioning cue that took Charlie back into his zone. The way it works is that through daily meditation or guided imagery, which I explain later, Charlie visualized himself being interviewed and talking about his creative work with the same confidence as Don Draper. I then asked Charlie to think of a cue to take him into that Don Draper confidence, which was his zone. It could be anything associated with Mad Men, but it had to be something he could think of without others knowing because he might use it during his interview. Anchors are most powerful when it's a physical gesture like putting your index finger and thumb together and every time you do that you connect that to an image and new story of success. For Charlie it could also be saying to himself the name Don Draper or Mad Men. It could be a mental image of Don Draper's office or home. It could be the *Mad Men* theme song. The important thing is that the gesture connects to the feeling and experience of success. Charlie immediately thought of Don Draper holding a glass of Scotch at work. There was a certain bravado that was part of Charlie's attraction to embodying Don Draper. Charlie wanted to internally feel some of that bravado during his interview instead of fear and anxiety. So, every day Charlie meditated, he held his hand sideways and open as if he was holding a glass of Scotch. This was his anchor. As a coach, it's important that I not choose the anchor. Charlie had to choose the anchor because it had to have meaning for him. Of course an anchor won't take you into your zone after just one or two repetitions, but after repeatedly doing it multiple times a day over successive days it became a helpful conditioning cue. The more he practiced, the faster Charlie could feel more confident and relaxed with an inner bravado.

GETTING INTO YOUR ZONE: THE POWER OF MINDSET, FOCUS, AND ENERGY LEVEL

Mindset is one of three critical forces that have to come together for you to get into your zone. Pam Brill's great book, *The Winner's Way*, clearly lays out these three forces. I'm simplifying what Dr. Brill says, but along with mindset, the other two forces are focus and energy level, or what Dr. Brill calls "Activation Level."

To demonstrate how these forces work together, let's do an exercise to get you into your zone. First of all, describe what the biggest, most meaningful success in your career was and what it felt like. If you have years of work experience and you don't feel like you've had a big success, then you're probably being too hard on yourself. Think about it more deeply. Haven't you done work that's benefitted other people or your company? Virtually everyone realizes they have with more reflection.

If you're a recent college graduate and don't feel like you have a successful career example yet, please think through internships or volunteering you've done in the past. Another example could be from a success you previously had in another area of your life. For example, were you ever part of a sports team that won a big game? Or perhaps you gave a special dance recital or maybe you're a musician who gave an excellent performance.

I asked Charlie this question and he said that one of his most memorable successes was when he was working at a website design agency. He was on the creative team and he presented his design to a client who absolutely loved it. He knew he was good, but until he saw the excited response from the client his confidence didn't match his creative abilities. Think about your own successful experience that has deep meaning for you as you answer these questions below.

Mindset

Exercise: Describe what your mindset was like during that experience? For example, did you feel confident, determined?

When I asked Charlie this question he said that when he was creating the new website design his mindset was confident and he was doing exactly what he was best at. He felt positive and creative. Charlie knew that his job title was "designer" but he always viewed himself as an artist. He felt his greatest strength was in creating designs that were both artistic and achieved the functional goals of the client. He felt like he was doing that as he came up with each new draft and he hoped the client would "get it."

Focus

In order to excel, you must be completely dedicated to your chosen sport. You must also be prepared to work hard and be willing to accept constructive criticism. Without a total 100 percent dedication, you won't be able to do this.

Willie Mays, Hall of Fame Baseball Player

Exercise: Thinking back to a great success you've had, describe what your focus felt like. Think about how dedicated you were in that experience. For example, did you feel like you had clarity of vision, a laser focus, a clear mind, no distractions?

A lack of focus has negative consequences. Most of us multitask and no one more than working parents, but our performance drops when we multitask as explained in this interesting *Men's Health* article.

Lack of focus decreases our performance in all areas of our life. Driving while distracted is dangerous with 25% of all accidents in America caused by people talking on their phones. Tiger Woods was unstoppable in his career until his personal life imploded, causing multiple distractions for arguably the greatest golfer the game has ever known. Tiger won fourteen major golf tournaments before his distracting scandals came out and he's won zero since.

When Charlie was creating his website design he felt "totally dialed in" and "almost possessed." He couldn't tell if he was driving his design or if it was emerging out of him. Either way, he was obsessed with continuously improving his design and found himself waking up in the middle of the night with new ideas.

Energy Level

Exercise: Describe what your energy level felt like during your big success. By energy level I mean your physiological state. For example, did you feel excited, a little nervous, calm, relaxed?

If one's energy level is too high they can psych themselves out or "choke" like we see professional athletes do all the time. If during an interview one's energy level is too low the applicant can seem disengaged and apathetic, and that's equally as negative as psyching one's self out. Find your "right" energy level—the one you were in when you performed at your highest levels in the past. As Author Pamela Brill explains, "activation" is your "physical and physiological experience at any moment…It has a significant impact on your ability to engage with challenges and do your best. The best-fit activation for any moment is not one-size-fits-all. Instead it is both situational and personal and affected by your activation style."

When he designed his highly successful website, Charlie described his energy level as "relaxed, almost meditative." He had learned that it was difficult for him to design at work because the buzz of the agency amped him up too much and took his energy level higher than his ideal state for designing. Also, he was often interrupted by well-meaning colleagues who had random questions or just wanted to tell Charlie about a party they were at over the weekend. So, he had developed the habit of working out of a quieter cafe a block away. That more relaxing environment was best for his ideal energy level and creativity.

Create From Your Future to Optimize Your Mindset

Another technique I recommend to optimize mindset is one I learned from the outstanding business coach, Rita Hovakimian. Every January I go through a personal planning workshop led by Rita to clarify my annual career and personal goals. She asks us to "write a story that captures your successful outcomes." By customizing Rita's technique for Charlie, I asked him to visualize himself one year in the future after getting this creative job. I asked him to answer questions like: What kinds of clients do you serve (large, small, healthcare, tech…)? What are your clients' responses to your creative work (i.e., appreciative, grateful)? How fulfilling is your job on a daily basis? What does it feel like to be established as a trusted member of the creative team that people sought out for ideas? Charlie also described his feelings of confidence and calm now that he was part of an agency that valued him—at the same time he was building greater financial security doing what he loved.

I personally do this visioning exercise every January in Rita's workshop and I update it during the year. I create from my future, one year out and three years out. As a result I gain clarity on my personal and career objectives. And it is beneficial for my mindset, too, since I find that it lowers my stress when I feel like I've already achieved my goals. That way I focus more on the fruit I've created instead of just thinking about the hard work of planting and gardening I have to do. I'd rather eat a plum than plant a seedling.

Manage Your Inner Critic

Even if you've come up with your old and new metaphors and you've done the work on your mindset, focus, and energy level, you may have some internal objection. This inner voice may be small or it may be screaming at you. If you're hearing this self-criticism you're probably hearing your inner critic. Your inner critic is your inner voice of doubt when you're not feeling confident or when you're experiencing low self-esteem.

We all have an inner critic and we all experience doubt at times. For some people their inner critic is small and infrequent. But for some people their inner critic is large, loud, and frequent—and that can cause real problems by preventing them from applying for a job because their inner critic is focused on the 10% of the job requirements they don't have experience with instead of the 90% they do. It also tries to make us think we're not smart enough or competent enough to achieve something. We may not go for that promotion because our inner critic says we won't succeed in it. It can sabotage our confidence and our career advancement as a result.

There's a great book I want to recommend called *Self Therapy for Your Inner Critic* by Jay Early and Bonnie Weiss. In it they describe how people are surprised to learn that at times their inner critic may be trying to help them by protecting them. The inner critic criticizes one's self and counsels them not to apply for that promotion so he or she won't risk failing. But as the authors point out, there's risk in anything we do.

You may be able to turn your inner critic into your inner champion. But if our inner critic is acting in a particularly harmful way we may have to overmatch it by yelling at it to go to hell. Don't let it prevent you from taking positive steps in your career. Understand that feeling low self-esteem can be the result of an inner critic attack, but it's not the truth of who you are. I'm a recovering perfectionist and I hate making mistakes, which makes my life opportunity-rich for my inner critic given that I make mistakes all the time. One way I've come to be more accepting of my mistakes is through Improv (improvisation comedy), which is the act of creating a scene with zero preparation. I'm currently taking my fifth Improv class at the fantastic BATS Improv here in San Francisco. If you haven't taken Improv before I highly recommend it, especially for fellow perfectionists because there's inherently a high failure rate in Improv. It's viewed that if you're not failing in Improv you're not taking risks. As a result of failing during each class I've become much more accepting of my mistakes, and that allows me to stay in my zone more often in business.

In addition to our inner critic we also have our intuition. People often confuse the two, but they are fundamentally different. Intuition is our ability to understand something immediately even if it's happening at the unconscious level. Many professionals have such a loud, relentless inner critic that it can drown out their intuition. Even though intuition can be wrong, you don't want your inner critic to be so loud that it silences your intuition, because intuition, combined with the analysis I detail in numerous steps throughout this book, leads to better career decision making.

Habits to Bring Your Mindset, Focus, and Energy Level Together Mindfully

Now that you've hopefully quieted your inner critic, you can use these techniques below to harness the power of your mindset, focus, and energy level in a mindful way. I truly use all of them every week, but you don't have to. Think of them as a tool kit. Try them all, use the ones that serve you and ignore the rest.

Exercising: This is the most obvious habit. Do whatever you enjoy the most that raises your heart beat. This can be anything from a thirty-minute fast walk to a high cardio workout. I swim regularly and meditate while I swim. I also get exercise from being an Argentine tango dancer for seven years. Dance has multiple benefits. Of course there's the added benefit of getting to hold lovely women in a close embrace for an evening. I just competed in the Argentine Tango USA Championship again with my fantastic Japanese partner. Tango has been amazingly beneficial for my mindset and health because I'm exercising without feeling like I'm working out. I only feel joy. The antidepressant benefits of exercise are well known, too. I interviewed a neuroscientist who is an expert in human performance and she told me that yoga is particularly beneficial for multiple reasons. An article by another neuroscientist describes how yoga can change the brain's stressful habits.

- Meditating: In addition to exercising, I've had clients tell me that of all the new habits they've added, doing daily meditation was the most beneficial for them. If you haven't tried meditating before, here's a fun video to introduce you to it.

- Meditation podcast: If you prefer listening to a meditation example instead of watching one, here's a podcast from Wendy Palmer, the principal and founder of the groundbreaking Leadership Embodiment.

- Meditation in text: If you prefer reading about meditation instead of watching or listening, here are three breathing exercises from Dr. Weil, the Integrative Medicine thought leader.

- Watching meditation videos. To supplement my sitting meditation practice I also watch a variety of meditation videos I've shot over the years on my phone. Here's the link to one that I shot of a beautiful, calming river running through the extraordinary Yosemite Valley during Thanksgiving weekend.

- If meditation isn't for you, there are a number of other relaxation techniques you can use, as listed by Dr. Mark Hyman, the health leader and bestselling author, in his informative post.

How can you argue with Doctor Hyman's prescriptions when one of them is to make love? Doctor's orders.

- Guided imagery: This requires a longer explanation, so please see my section in this chapter on Guided Imagery.

- Power poses: I'm always learning on Ted.com and one of my favorite talks is by Amy Cuddy and her work on "power posing," which I've adopted and encourage others to use. Amy Cuddy is a professor at Harvard Business School and one of her areas of research, according to Ted.com, is "how your body position influences others and even your own brain". I do weekly radio interviews that are often early in the morning. When I get up that early after a night of tango dancing I'm feeling foggy, but I have to be clear-minded and confident while being interviewed. So I do power poses for a couple of minutes before the radio host calls me and it helps me get into my zone. I also coach people on using power poses before walking into an interview to increase their confidence and decrease their cortisol levels.

- EFT: "Tapping technique." Deepak Chopra has said, "EFT offers great healing benefits." I don't know if there's science behind this, but I do it and always feel more relaxed afterwards.

The Power of Guided Imagery for Your Mindset

Guided imagery is a technique that uses positive mental images in order to achieve a particular goal and I recommend it for some career coaching clients. It's becoming increasingly common in hospitals nationally, which use guided imagery with patients in pre and post-operative stages of surgery to reduce pain and manage anxiety. It's also been proven to reduce recovery time.

To experience it yourself, I recommend watching the video of Dr. Martin Rossman leading a guided imagery session. Another option is that you can do guided imagery by yourself as expertly explained by Leslie Davenport, one of America's thought leaders in guided imagery and its use in healthcare. You can also work with a guided imagery practitioner who can lead you through the experience. I've done over a dozen guided imagery sessions with an excellent professional practitioner, Amanda Pirot, and it's been surprisingly beneficial for me in a variety of ways. I used it when I was leading a project to create a new brand. This was a brand I had been living and breathing for over six months. I literally dreamt about the brand, so, frankly, I was skeptical that guided imagery could unearth anything in my mind I hadn't already thought of. But during my session I had deeper insight into the brand and what it would mean to customers than I'd ever had before, which proved incredibly valuable. I've also done sessions to reduce stress and anxiety and it truly worked. And I've used guided imagery to increase my performance and focus. I realized years ago that I perform at my highest level when I'm totally focused. During one of my sessions I accessed a more powerful understanding of my focus and had an image of a "blue laser of focus" shooting out of my eyes. Since that day when I meditate I always think of my "blue laser of focus" and it helps me clear my mind of meaningless distractions and focus on what's important.

Here's a simple overview of how you can use guided imagery when you have an upcoming job interview:

- Spend 10-15 minutes clearing your mind and relaxing.
    - Visualize your interview going successfully from start to finish. Visualize yourself in your office space talking to your future colleagues. Visualize successfully handling all difficult questions and then getting that job offer.
    - How do you feel? Are you excited to be there? Do you feel confident, calm or nervous?
    - What details do you see? Imagine the friendly face of the hiring manager.
    - What sounds do you hear? Do you hear the hum of the office around you?
    - If you have any mental blocks or anxieties pop up,visualize yourself working through these issues and still successfully achieving your goal.

- Ask a wise person or inner career guide what advice they have for you to achieve your goal. For example, one time I was preparing for an interview and I visualized Bill Clinton appearing as my inner guide because President Clinton is a master at answering any question. I imagined him giving me tips on how to answer interview questions.

- Ask that wise person or inner guide to give you something to remember this visualization by. During my visualization I saw Bill Clinton giving me a Gold Star like a teacher gives a student for a job well done.

- After you finish your visualization, write a short story summarizing all the positives you have just visualized. I save these notes so I can refer back to them later. You can also put photos, images, or video on your phone to remind you of your own success. By doing guided imagery you should feel greater confidence and lower anxiety about your job interview or any other career goal you're focused on achieving.

- Do this visualization every day leading up to your interview and do it the morning of your interview, too.

- I use guided imagery for more than specific short-term career goals. The workshops I do with Rita Hovakimian include completing a three-year visualization. I then break my three year and one year goals into short-term goals that allow me to achieve my longer term goals. Of course priorities in life change over time, and when they do for me I simply update my goals during the year. I always carry my goals with me, which allows me to stay focused and in my optimal mindset.

I offer these techniques as options for you to consider making into habits. Aside from the obvious multiple benefits of exercise, I'm not attached to any of these techniques for you.

Swimming may be your favorite exercise. You may also find it meditative and that it allows you to go into your zone. You may feel awkward doing guided imagery, power poses, or the tapping technique. That's totally fine. I'm simply suggesting these as options for you to use. Try them all, keep the ones that benefit you, make them into habits and discard the rest.

If you've done everything I've listed in this chapter you should now be able to enter your optimal mindset. Of course you cannot stay in your zone 24/7 but you have an understanding now about how you are best able to use these habits to go back into your zone. To further develop your mindset, there's a summary of an excellent article in the March/April 2013 issue of *Scientific American Mind* about mindfulness I recommend.

Your confidence is increasing. You are more relaxed. You have clarity of focus. Your stress and anxiety levels are decreasing. Now that you have mastered your mindset let's move to Step Two where I'll guide you through how to optimize your personal ecosystem.

Summary

Step One. Chapter 1: Optimizing your mindset is your critical first step to getting hired. If you're not in your zone, your job search will take longer and you'll be less likely of finding a fulfilling job.

- You control most of getting hired.
- Don't try to block or ignore your inner critic. Start working on transforming it into your inner champion.

Techniques to optimize your mindset:

- Create your old metaphor and your new metaphor.
- Create your anchor to return to your zone.
- To go into your zone do the chapter exercises to find your optimal mindset, focus and energy level.
- Complete the "Create from your future" chapter exercise.
- Regularly exercise, meditate, watch meditation videos, do guided imagery, try power poses, and try the EFT "tapping technique." Keep the habits that benefit you. Discard the rest.

Step Two: Optimize Your Personal Ecosystem

Get hired for a job that's an excellent fit by your ideal company and boss with this step-by-step plan.

When you accept a new job you haven't just joined a new company, you've joined a new ecosystem. Think of this new ecosystem as a body—a system that interacts with its various parts and interconnects people throughout your company. I've seen new employees join a company and not fit in. When this happens there's organ rejection and the employee isn't at the company much longer. So, keep in mind that there are numerous factors in your new ecosystem affecting your success. There's your mindset, your performance in the job you were hired to do, your team's performance, your relationship with your boss and their boss, your relationships with the people on your team or division, the connections you build with people throughout your organization and with vendors, and how much you "fit" into your company culture. The better you fit into your new ecosystem and the healthier your ecosystem, the more successful you and your new organization will be.

If you have two job offers then you are evaluating two completely different ecosystems. Company A might have a boss you'd love working for in a company culture you find tolerable. Company B might have a boss that would annoy you to no end in a culture you find more inspirational than any in which you've ever worked. Company C might have a boss and company culture you like but where you'll have a direct report who got passed over for the team leader job you just got. That direct report may have made a secret vow to do everything in his power to sabotage your every move in ways that make antics on *The Office* look like child's play. All three ecosystems will affect your performance and quality of life in different ways.

After I finished graduate school I moved to magical Prague where I learned a lot about ecosystems. During my six years there I turned around Anglo-American University (AAU) with four colleagues in the early 1990s. The university was on the verge of closing down and most people thought we were going to fail. Early on when I was teaching a marketing class, I remember asking the visionary founder if he thought the university was going to survive and he said he didn't know. The university was virtually bankrupt and had dropped from 120 down to 60 students, but the students that remained were an integral part of our ecosystem because they were very smart, ambitious, and highly committed to making the university succeed. The teachers were equally committed as proven by the fact they taught for a pittance. My colleagues and I took a leap of faith and decided to try and lead the turnaround of the university. I became the chairman of the Business and Economics School and we all began the next phase of the university's journey. A few years later the university was financially stable and had over 300 students. That turnaround happened because of our ecosystem: We had outstanding students who wanted to learn in a new educational environment, one that "combined the best of American and British academic principles with Central European traditions"; we had excellent teachers and management who wanted to contribute to the further building of an educational institution; we had a strong band of Country Managers of multinational corporations such as Colgate-Palmolive, AIG, Citibank and SC Johnson, who gave financial support to the university when nobody else would. They also provided strong leadership as Board members. And we had generous facility support from the local Prague government who provided us with our first campus. If there had been even one weak part in our ecosystem the university would've closed forever. Instead, it rebounded and years after my colleagues and I left a new generation of leaders took it to greater achievement as it became the first private university accredited in the Czech Republic. For years now it has been very successful and it has grown to over 500 impressive students. AAU offers an excellent, diverse education and, thanks to the Knights of Malta, the students study in a restored 18th century palace one block from the Charles Bridge. AAU has risen to heights we only dreamed of twenty years ago.

Why did all of us involved in the turnaround of the university take the leap of faith? We trusted the health of our ecosystem. We knew it was a once-in-a-lifetime opportunity to contribute to the education of admirable students in an extraordinary country that had recently emerged from Communist rule. And we knew ourselves.

Chapter 2: How to Know Yourself: 5 Methods to Greater Self-Awareness

Steve had been working in PR for over fifteen years and he was good at it. He was a very good, if not great, writer; he usually hit his deadlines, and his colleagues and clients liked him. There was just one problem. He didn't find his job exciting anymore and he was increasingly bored. In his early years in PR he got a rush whenever one of his press releases was picked up by media. He found it even more exciting to come up with some creative campaign that was referenced in The New York Times. Those days were long gone. But it was a comfortable routine for him and he had to pay the bills, so he kept doing it day after day even though he'd been on autopilot for over three years.

His boss could tell something was different, but he hadn't confronted Steve because he was doing a good, if not excellent, job. Plus, his boss had to deal with the squeaky wheels that were the problem children on their team and Steve was able to continue to skate as a result. Steve hadn't made the conscious decision yet to transition to a new career, but he knew at an unconscious level a simple truth: He was deeply unfulfilled and he couldn't go on like that.

Often we coach people who have plateaued and they're not sure why. They feel like they were on a fast track five years ago and somehow they ended up on a slow track. They're not even sure when it happened. They just know they've lost something that they want to get back. Inertia has set into their lives and fossilized their careers. People stay in a job because they don't think they have another choice. In fact, they have multiple choices.

The key to figuring out what direction to aim is finding the intersection of your passion, your expertise, and opportunities. The healthier the ecosystem you join, the more you'll achieve on the spectrum of your success.

Think about Tom Brady, the quarterback for the New England Patriots. He's had all of these factors working for him in his ecosystem for years and that's led to winning more playoff games than any other quarterback in NFL history. He's passionate about what he does, he has expertise in his job as an elite quarterback, he's on the right team (company), and he has the right boss in Coach Belichik. He was the backup quarterback who got his opportunity when the starting quarterback was seriously injured. If just one of those factors in his personal ecosystem were different, such as trying something silly like playing running back, he wouldn't have been so incredibly successful. In corporate terms we'd consider Tom Brady a "high performer" and their success often travels well across organizations. We saw that with Peyton Manning, another elite quarterback, who was not re-signed by the Indianapolis Colts and ended up joining the Denver Broncos. Manning had an excellent year and nearly made the AFC Championship game. But the Broncos were a healthy ecosystem before Manning joined them and he made them better. If Brady or Manning were to join an unhealthy ecosystem like the Jacksonville Jaguars, it's unlikely either high performer could make them better than an average team without other parts of the ecosystem getting healthier.

What ecosystem do you thrive best in? Let's start with your passion. What energizes you? How can you know what direction to move towards for your job search if you don't know what moves you?

HERE'S HOW YOU CAN IDENTIFY YOUR PASSION:

1. **Self-awareness exercises for one or two weeks.** In coaching and in life, self-awareness is critical. So, start journaling for ten to fifteen minutes on a daily basis. After you write whatever is top of mind, answer these questions: What do you love about your current/last job? What frustrated you in your last job? What kind of job do you want next? If you could create your ideal job description, what would it say? What kind of work/life balance do you want? What are your career goals? If you could have any job and every job paid the same what would you choose? As you do these self-awareness exercises don't limit your thinking only to your current career. Oftentimes the thing we're most passionate about isn't how we're currently making our living, it's a hobby we're insanely passionate about that should be our career.

2. **Assessment testing:** If you haven't done self-assessment testing before, this is a great place to start. I've taken every one listed below and I've gotten different insights from each, so it really depends on your goals. The value in taking them is that you gain a better understanding of your strengths and interests, so you have a direction to point for your job search. There are numerous self-assessment tests out there that are insightful, so I'm just summarizing some of the most popular here with copy from their respective websites:

   - Birkman: I've taken this test and it's one of my favorites. "The Birkman Method personality test accurately measures productive behaviors, stress behaviors, underlying needs, motivations, and organizational orientation."

   - Myers Briggs. The Myers Briggs Type Indicator (MBTI) identifies and describes sixteen different personality types.

- DiSC: The DiSC test centers around four different personality traits: Dominance, Inducement, Submission, and Compliance.

- StrengthsFinder: I love this test because of its philosophy that in our careers it's best to focus on our strengths. Created by Gallup, StrengthsFinder helps you discover your top five talents.

- Enneagram: Also highly thought of, the Enneagram shows you which of nine distinct personality types you have and what that means for your life: The Reformer, The Helper, The Achiever, The Individualist, The Investigator, The Loyalist, The Enthusiast, The Challenger, and The Peacemaker.

Many of these assessments are expensive, so if you're currently employed, ask your company if they'll pay for it. If you're a student, ask your university if they offer free self-assessment testing. If none of these are options for you, you can take a DiSC assessment for free by going to TonyRobbins.com. On his site you'll search for the keyword "assessment" and you'll see a link to a free DiSC assessment. (Please note I have no relationship with TonyRobbins.com.) I've taken it and it's insightful. I had to give some contact information such as email and phone, to be able to take the assessment for free. Naturally, they're using it as a lead generation tool for their company, but TonyRobbins.com has been professional in using that information. I've only gotten a few emails and they've never phoned me. Taking the DiSC will show you what kind of insight into yourself you'll get. That'll help you decide if that's enough for you or if you want to pay for another assessment.

3. **Ask friends and family for feedback.** How many people know us as well as our friends and family do? And yet, often we don't ask them for feedback. Sure, Mom will give us plenty of advice, requested or not, about dating, parenting etc., but have you gotten her feedback, or Dad's, or your sibling's or best friend's on key questions like: What am I best at in any area of my life? What do I think I'm good at but actually I'm not? What do you believe I am most passionate about in any area of my life? Just like in the self-assessment section earlier in this chapter, don't limit these questions only to your career. Get feedback on all parts of your life. Asking these questions can feel awkward at first because it's often challenging to hear feedback about ourselves. That's why it's important to start with the person you trust the most and go on from there. To ask a trusted family member or friend for feedback simply tell them you're trying to better understand yourself and that the most helpful thing they can do is be totally honest with you. After you get their feedback, treat it like feedback you would get in an annual performance review. Don't dispute it; don't argue against it. Feel free to ask clarifying questions, but otherwise take the feedback without response and let it sink in so you can reflect upon it.

4. **Do a 360 assessment test:** Of all the things I've done in my career, one of the most valuable was receiving a 360 assessment. A 360 provides feedback on a variety of job-related areas from a "full circle" of directions including the boss, direct reports, and peers. 360s are primarily used for development, not performance assessment, and thus provide a wealth of valuable information that can be useful without feeling our job is in jeopardy. My 360 confirmed some positive things I expected and it showed me areas where I needed to improve, which helped drive my development plan the following year.

5. **Look at your Internet surfing history:** We are what we do, so most likely the sites we spend the most time on will reveal areas in our lives that we're passionate about. Of course we do some surfing for entertainment and it may not have anything to do with a possible career path. I go to ESPN.com and TheOnion.com most days, but I don't have a desire to be a sports or satirical writer—I do it to follow my favorite teams and to read something funny. But in tracking my time online I also saw that I spend a lot of evenings on TED.com—and that made a lot of sense, given my passion for learning. What sites do you spend most of your time on? Based on your surfing history, what jobs might be of interest for you?

Passion is a great start, but it isn't enough. I'm passionate about soccer, but I'm never going to be play in the English Premier League. You need expertise, too.

To know if you have a skill set that matches your passion, ask yourself these questions and take these actions to gain greater insight into what you are excellent at:

- Do a self-evaluation of your work and see if it matches what your boss's performance review says. For example, if your company doesn't already do this, before receiving your annual performance review from your boss, evaluate yourself using the same form. Answer all the key questions evaluating your leadership skills, analytical skills, presentation skills, etc. Also evaluate yourself on how many of your objectives you successfully completed. Afterwards, compare your self-review versus the review your boss gave you to see what "areas of improvement" you missed. Additionally, write out what you believe are your greatest strengths. It's also important to know your weaknesses so that you can either focus your career on your strengths or work to improve your weaknesses. These lists can be a starting point for feedback you also get from family, friends, and trusted co-workers. Absorb the feedback and create a development plan out of it.

- If you're a recent college graduate with little or no work experience, or if you're unemployed and won't be getting a performance review, you can do a "career pathing" exercise instead. Career pathing is the process where you identify the next job you'd like to have and then create a development plan to achieve that role. Career pathing includes understanding the mindset, skill set, knowledge, and personal characteristics you need to get your target job. Be brutally honest with yourself. Maybe you want to get a job as a financial analyst. You may have graduated with a degree in finance and have a very analytical mind, but realize the career path you want requires completing the Chartered Financial Analyst (CFA) program.

- StrengthsFinder (StrengthsFinder.com): You can read the book "StrengthsFinder" or you can go to gallupstrengthsfinder.com to take the test, which is currently $9.99.

Ask friends and family for feedback. This has some similarities to doing a self-evaluation and comparing it to your performance review. But it's different in two key ways because: (a) You're getting feedback from people who know you best versus a new boss who may have known you for eight weeks and (b) your boss is obviously focused on reviewing your work performance, which your family may know little about. When I was thinking about starting another company I talked to my parents, my brother and sister, as well as my closest friends. To a person, they all thought I was well suited to create because it matched my passion and skill set. That feedback was a tipping point for me and convinced me I was on the right track.

- Take tests to measure your level of excellence. For example, I coached a manager who was moving into online marketing and he wanted to focus on search engine marketing (SEM). He took online tests via the Google Certification Program and this allowed him to know what SEM skills he was proficient at and what skills he still needed to improve. Likewise, there are multiple educational sites today that are free such as TED.com, KhanAcademy.org and Saylor.org. Saylor is actually a "free and open collection of college courses" that offers over 250 free courses. Do you need to bone up on statistics for your job? Take a free class on Saylor.org and take the final exam at the end to know if you've become proficient. Moreover, there are now public universities that have started offering free courses for credit.

- Ask vendors you work with. At one company where I was previously employed, I worked with a leading online marketing vendor. Towards the end of the project I asked the vendor to give me an honest appraisal of my skills. It turned out I was stronger in SEO and weaker in SEM than I realized. This feedback was tremendously valuable for me and, as a result, I spent the next year improving my SEM skills.

- Talk to recruiters when appropriate. I have an entire chapter later in the book on working with recruiters.

- Give presentations or teach. When I lived in Prague I taught for over five years and I didn't know until then exactly where in marketing I had expertise and where I didn't. Thousands of questions from students will give you that clarity.

- Build your presence on social media, by blogging or becoming active on Facebook, Twitter, Linkedin, etc. Then evaluate the feedback you get: Are you able to build a community or not? In a later chapter I focus on Linkedin.

- Get involved in your local industry organizations. Over the past seven months I've been active in the amazing Northern California Human Resources Association (NCHRA) where I've not only learned a lot about other HR topics and built many new connections, but I've also developed a greater understanding of where my expertise lies. There are all kinds of industry/trade groups you can benefit from and the obvious ones are often not the only choices. Expanding your options and experiencing different events will open your opportunities, too.

The other critical factor in figuring out what direction to drive towards is to determine what jobs are in strong and growing demand. Fortunately, there are more ways to determine that than ever:

- Get salary data for your job type in your market. It's critical to do this before you negotiate salary because you have to know what the market rate is. You may have some contacts at your target company who will tell you their salary range. Some people when asked their salary range will look at you as if you've just said their dog is ugly, so typically it's just friends who may be open to sharing this information. I've been a member of a career group for over ten years (more on that later) and we share this information openly, but we're all friends who have built up a lot of trust over the years. If you have a target company and you're already talking to a recruiter for that company you can ask the recruiter. You can also use sites such as Salary.com and Glassdoor.com to get self-reported data, which is a great starting point. Job postings by companies on CraigsList.org will sometimes list the salary they're offering.

- Talk to your friends and your contacts, such as former colleagues, and ask them which jobs are most in demand. When I was first approached by a recruiter about working at CREDO Mobile, I was interested first and foremost because of its progressive mission. But when I talked to my friends about the idea of applying they all talked about how hot mobile was becoming and how valuable that would be for me in the next three to five years of my career.

- Talk to recruiters. When you talk to recruiters ask them "How's the market?" to keep your finger on the pulse of the job market. I have an entire chapter later on what to focus on when talking to recruiters.

Even if you're in a highly competitive market like law, the goal is to find a niche that is in high demand. For example, I worked with an intellectual property (IP) lawyer who was contracting at a previous company and I'd only see him face-to-face every couple of months. He had built up unique IP expertise in a certain type of mobile technology. As a result, even in a tough market for many lawyers overall, he is constantly in high demand, able to charge jaw-dropping hourly rates and he works from whatever awesome locations around the world he wants.

You've optimized your mindset. You're evaluating your strengths and what kind of ecosystem you'll best fit into. But that's only part of your ecosystem. Knowing your future company and its culture is also critical to thriving.

Summary

Step Two: Optimize Your Personal Ecosystem. When you accept an offer you're not just taking a job. You're entering an ecosystem. The better you perform and the healthier your ecosystem the greater your chances of success.

Chapter 2: How to Know Yourself. Your success and healthy mindset starts with knowing yourself. Five methods to greater self-awareness include:

- Self-awareness exercises for 1-2 weeks.
- Assessment testing.
- Asking friends and family for feedback.
- Doing a 360 assessment test when possible.
- Looking at your internet surfing history.

Chapter 3: How to Determine Your Ideal Company and Culture Fit

I'd only been working at AllAdvantage, an Internet startup, for a few weeks but it was exhilarating. Everything seemed possible. I felt lucky to be there and everyone believed we were building what would become a massive Internet success, which explained why most of us worked until 7pm, 8pm, 9pm... We didn't care—there wasn't any place we'd rather be than creating a new Internet category that we believed was going to provide great value to customers.

The speed of our growth and crash was stunning. I was roughly employee number 60. A year later we had over 800 employees and a year after that there were zero employees. The company raised and then burned through $175 million in venture capital funding.

During our ride up we had a unique culture that attracted applicants with varying motivations. One man said he wanted to work at the company so he could make a lot of money if we went public. He wasn't hired. Another applicant said "There's a party going on here and I want to be part of it." He was hired immediately. Even though the company was only recently founded, there quickly developed an "AllAdvantage way" of doing things and one of those cultural values was speed.

As fast-moving as the culture was, we balanced that with a lot of fun with ping-pong and foosball tournaments, free dinners and soccer games during lunch. One friend even painted his car AllAdvantage purple.

Certainly AllAdvantage is a dramatic example, but some people love the idea of working in such a culture. There are plenty of people, though, who would feel uncomfortable in that kind of culture and instead prefer one that is slowly evolving. There isn't a one-size-fits-all answer for cultural preference. Figuring out your cultural ideal is what's most important.

- Does rapid change excite you or do you prefer more cautious cultures?
- Do you prefer a freewheeling or process-focused environment?
- How important is it to you to work in a company where diversity is accepted and appreciated? There are broad generalizations that can be made about corporate cultures in different parts of the country, but please don't assume that your target company has a certain culture just because of where it's based or the industry it's in. There are cutting edge companies in every part of the country and in every industry, which is why it's so important to understand the unique culture of your target company.
- Flat organization or hierarchical? Do you want or care if there are multiple layers of management above you?
- Team oriented or very competitive? If you like a supportive culture you'll want more of a focus on team versus highly competitive organizations. Of course some companies are internally team oriented and externally highly competitive.
- Long working hours or more of a work/life balance? If you're married with children work/life balance can be of particular importance for you.

Once you have an understanding of your ideal culture you'll be able to target companies with that culture. Knowing if you'll fit into and excel in your future company's culture is critical to creating your successful ecosystem.

A lot of people spend more time researching their fantasy football team than they do understanding their preferred company culture or researching their target companies. I can count on one hand the number of people we've coached who do a thorough job researching target companies. Having experienced it myself after preparing intensely for an interview, I can tell you that employers are impressed when a candidate knows a lot about the company, their market, and when the candidate has insightful strategic recommendations. Most people focus more on the job itself and less on company culture. Unfortunately, what happens is that people take a job they think they're going to love, but end up feeling like they "don't fit in" with the new company culture.

And yet for most human resource leaders interviewing a candidate, it all comes down to two key questions:

1. Can they do the job?
2. Will they fit into the culture?

So, how do you research a company and its culture?

- Talk with current and past employees: Use Linkedin to find your first level connections and then call them up or take them to lunch to learn about the company culture.

- Online research: Linkedin and Glassdoor. Use Linkedin to get a snapshot of the company. Use Glassdoor to read the employee reviews of the company to see if the culture sounds like a fit for you. One little-known feature on Glassdoor is their "Photos" tab. To see what I mean, go to Glassdoor.com, do a "Company" search for Google and then once you're on their page click on "Photos." You'll see over one hundred photos of Google offices around the world. This is just another reason why I love Glassdoor—this type of transparent feature gives you a better feel for Google's culture. I've been in Google's headquarters multiple times for industry events and these photos do a great job of capturing the fun, cool feeling of their offices.

- Annual reports and industry reports: Annual reports give you an abundance of information about the company and its culture. Is the annual report boring and dry? Their culture probably is, too. Hoovers.com has excellent company and industry reports where you can get detailed company information (history, executive bios, competitors...) and industry information (trends, growth rates...). Do the executives sound like they have inspiring backgrounds to you?

- Do an Internet search for "Company name, ratings & reviews". I always do this. Once I was preparing for my interview with the CEO of a company and I did this Internet search. To my surprise I found many customer complaints and many of them seemed to be legitimately calling into question the business practices of the company. I asked the CEO about this when we spoke and his response was not convincing. So, I withdrew my candidacy and never looked back. About a year later I talked to a friend who told me he had a friend who went to work at the same company, but quit after two months because he didn't agree with the company's business practices.

- And you need to interview them, too. When you go in for your round of interviews they're not just interviewing you—you're screening them, too. Ask the people you meet with to describe the culture. Does it sound like a culture you'd be excited to join? Are the employees consistently describing the culture in the same way? If not, it's probably a culture in flux and that can be difficult to navigate. Yahoo, for example, was one of the earliest stars of the Internet, grew very successfully, and then went through rough years and multiple CEOs. Their new CEO, Marissa Meyer seems to be off to a good start and by all accounts and Glassdoor reviews morale has improved. There's been controversy regarding the recent policy that eliminated working from home. So, if you're interviewing a company in flux like Yahoo you'd want to interview them, too, to get a better sense of how rapidly they're turning around and then decide if that's a great cultural fit for you.

- Ask yourself one of Warren Buffett's litmus test questions: Does the company have an "enduring competitive advantage?" If not, do you have a compelling reason to join the company?

Let's assume your target company passes your litmus test for your ecosystem. It's equally important that you have the right kind of boss in order to thrive. You don't have to love your boss or ever want to have drinks with him. But there are critical success factors that must be in place that I explain next.

Summary

Chapter 3. Determining your ideal company and culture fit is critical to your success. To understand that:

- Describe your preferred company culture. Is it a hierarchical or flat organization? Is it highly competitive or collaborative? Does it change rapidly or slowly?

- Based on your ideal company culture, list your target companies.

To research a company and its culture use these methods:

- Talk with current and past employees.
- Do online research using key sites like Linkedin and Glassdoor. Also do an Internet search for “Company name, ratings & reviews”.
- Review annual reports and industry reports.
- Interview the company just like they’re interviewing you. The better the company the more impressed they’ll be by your strategic, respectful questions.

Chapter 4: How to Know Your Potential Boss

He's rude and abrasive.
She knows I'm drowning in work, but she doesn't care.
He steals credit for my work.
She doesn't have my back.
He kisses upwards, but kicks everyone underneath him.
She micromanages every single thing I do.
He's belittling to me, so I'm leaving the company.

Sound familiar? I hope not! But I'm afraid you've probably suffered through a bad boss before. Most of us have. I know I have, although not in years. Fortunately, most of my bosses were excellent for very different reasons. But having a bad boss brings out in us feelings from mild annoyance to daily pain.

Every quote at the top of this chapter is about a real boss from a real direct report. Of all the research you do on a company you might join, there's nothing as important as the research you do on your potential boss. Bosses are an essential part of your ecosystem. Learn as much about that person as possible before you take the job. I don't want you to make the mistake one woman made when she said, "My old boss was mediocre, but she was tolerable. I jumped to a new company thinking it was going to be so much better, but my new boss turned out to be a total jerk. I was too embarrassed to ask my old company if I could go back to them and I didn't feel like I could jump to another company so quickly—it would look bad on my resume. I felt stuck."

HERE ARE THE MOST COMMON QUESTIONS I RECEIVE FROM OUR CLIENTS ABOUT BOSSES

1. *As far as my career advancement is concerned, how important is my relationship with my boss?*

   It's critically important because it's the #1 reason people quit their jobs: "People leave managers not companies" (Gallup).

   And according to research done at Florida State University, "40% of employees work for bad bosses."

2. *I'd like to have a better relationship with my boss, so what can I do to build that kind of great working relationship with him or her?*

   Get to know their working style as quickly as possible.

   What's their communication style: Are they very direct, diplomatic, competitive, metrics-driven, story-driven, progress-driven, talkers...?

   Also, learn their communication preferences: Email, IM, face-to-face, phone, morning/evening?

3. *Given how important a great relationship with a boss can be, when I am interviewing for a new job, what kinds of things should I be looking for as both good and bad signs in a new boss?*

   You're interviewing them, too, so look for big things like: Will your boss have your back? Will they be straight with you? Will they be reasonable in their expectations? Are you comfortable with their values? This can be challenging to determine in a thirty minute interview, but it's amazing how much can be revealed. When I was living in Prague I interviewed for an executive role that would've paid me far more than I'd ever earned there. But during the one-hour interview with the founder he made two disparaging comments about other Central Europeans in the region and that offended me. I realized at that moment I couldn't work for this man. The executive recruiter called me afterwards to say the founder wanted to move forward with me. I told her I wasn't interested in doing that because I didn't feel a cultural fit with him. I've made plenty of mistakes in my career, but I've always viewed that decision as one of my best. I simply will not work for anyone I do not respect, regardless of how much they're paying me.

You should also look for little things like: Was she on time to your interview? Did she come in prepared, having already read your resume? If the answer is no to both of those questions, did she acknowledge this? Everyone is busy, but common courtesy still applies. If your future boss doesn't care about being late to their first meeting with you, then that tells you something about what they're going to be like as a boss.

It's for these reasons above that your future boss fits so importantly into your personal ecosystem. A great future boss will enable your success, not block it.

You now have skills and resources to better know yourself, your future company culture, and your future boss. But in getting hired you should never go it alone. Instead you want to take Step Three and build your dream team.

Summary

Chapter 4. According to Gallup, the #1 reason people quit their jobs is their manager. As Gallup said "people leave managers not companies." Knowing your potential boss is critical to your success.

- What's their communication style? Is it direct and to the point? Or do they like to ponder questions? Are they competitive? If so, you should position progress reports in comparison to your biggest competitors. Are they metrics-driven or story-driven?
- What are their communication preferences? Email, text, IM, phone, Skype or face-to-face?
- Will your boss have your back? If not, who will? Will they be straight with you? Will your boss be reasonable in their expectations or will you move heaven and earth for them only to have them express disappointment in your progress? Are you comfortable with their values?

Step Three: Build Your Dream Team

How to establish your own trusted circle of advisors, supporters, and mentors.

CHAPTER 5: HOW TO BUILD YOUR DREAM TEAM

What does virtually every Olympian and world-class athlete have in common?

What do Tom Brady, Lindsey Vonn and Rory McIlroy all have in common?

Every single one of these champions has a team supporting their success. They're not doing it alone. Without those teams, it would be very hard for them to be as successful as they are. Do you have your "dream team" around you to ensure your success?

Rory McIlroy has a swing coach, a putting coach, a trainer and dietician, and a caddy he relies on for on-course advice. He also gets tremendous support from his parents and usually one of them is at whichever tournament he's playing.

Imagine if we could be like Rory, who has a caddy he trusts and who gives him advice before big shots in tension-filled tournaments. Imagine if you had a trusted person like a caddy to help you carry the load and to talk to before every important decision at work. If you haven't done so already, put your great team together like Rory did. Use it to help you get hired, or if you're already at a company, use it to help you take your career to the next level.

HERE ARE THE MOST COMMON QUESTIONS THAT I RECEIVE FROM OUR CLIENTS ABOUT BUILDING A DREAM TEAM

1. *What is a career "dream team" and why do I need one?*

Your career team is a trusted circle of people you form to help you navigate your career, learn, and lean on when you need support, as we all do.
You help them, too. It's mutually beneficial.

2. *What benefits will I realize by having a great team?*

- Accountability: This comes from having a mentor or coach. You may let yourself down, but you're less likely to let your mentor or coach down. If you set a deadline with yourself to update your resume by Monday you're more likely to do that if you've made that promise to a mentor or coach.
- Emotional support: The fact is, at times we simply need to blow off steam or we need someone to give us positive encouragement when we're feeling down about our job or job search.

3. *Who should be on my dream team?*

- Mentors: Choose one or two you highly respect from previous companies or from your network. These are people who can be invaluable by helping you with your career pathing, lifelong learning, and support. I've had multiple mentors during my career and they have changed my life.
- Career group: Build a career group of six to eight people. I devote the entire next chapter to building and running your own career group.
- Your high school or university alumni group: Think about your most memorable moments in life. A number of them probably came from your high school and university experiences. And

yet we coach people all the time who are not involved in their local alumni association even though those contacts can be amazingly helpful. So, get involved—you have shared experiences with these people that graduates of other schools can't understand. And you'll have fun, too. I did my undergrad at the University of Florida, so I'm a Gator. I always try to respond to requests from fellow Gators. Sometimes, when I'm feeling particularly generous, I'll even help Dawgs and Seminoles, which is an inside joke my fellow college football fanatics will understand. I did my MBA at the Kellogg School at Northwestern University and I am always going to local events to learn, have fun, and make new connections. I recently taught Argentine tango at a dance party for Kellogg alumni and that was great fun. I'm also the Career Affinity Chair for the Kellogg alumni group in the Bay Area, which allows me to help people in their professional development as well as raise awareness

Professional networking groups: For the past couple of years I've been a member of the Marketing Executives Networking Group (MENG) and it's excellent. We meet regularly to learn, network, hear war stories, and learn best practices. We also share which vendors are great and which ones to avoid. What industry group can you join?

Career coach: My company, is a coaching group. I've received invaluable feedback from coaches I've worked with over the years, which is part of the reason I started. I walk the talk, too, as over the past six months I've been coached by an outstanding executive coach who also has expertise in conflict resolution, Toma Ramirez. His coaching has significantly benefited me. Think about the areas in your career where you might benefit from having a sounding board. We also coach clients on navigating their career path, increasing productivity, conflict resolution, and reducing stress and anxiety, among other issues. The main way a coach differs from a mentor is that you typically pay for coaching, but you don't pay mentors.

- Make at least one friend at work. According to Gallup research we're more likely to stay at a company if we have a friend there. A trusted friend at work can be a great sounding board for you, help you learn the culture, and provide support.

- Friends and family: Having positive, loving support during challenging times is important. If you can't count on anyone else during tough times you should be able to count on your best friends and family.

- Physical trainer: The benefits of exercise are clear scientifically. Exercise is also an excellent anti-depressant. It doesn't matter if you lift weights, work with a yoga instructor, dance teacher, or swim buddy. The important thing is to exercise at least three times a week.

- Learning and development outside of work: Push the edges of your creative envelope by learning new skills. I've taken five Improv classes (Improv.org) over the past eighteen months and it's been amazingly fun! And, to my surprise, Improv has also taught me a number of life lessons: "Accept all offers," as opposed to saying "no" to everything; "make your partner look good," which is great for the weekly radio interviews I do on career topics. I've also been studying Argentine tango for seven years, which has been great fun and a super way to meet interesting people. And I've done over ten guided imagery sessions to help me visualize the company I wanted to build. Every January I do a "personal visioning" workshop where I plan for my year. What new skill can you learn this year?

4. *What if I can't afford to pay them?*

   You don't need to pay anything for most of them: Mentors, career groups, alumni associations, a friend at work, family and friends …

5. *Would it be smart for me to try to get on the dream teams of others?*

   Yes, because that's a way you can give back to all the benefits we've received from mentoring. As the saying goes, "Givers gain."

6. *Are there any pitfalls to avoid in building my dream team?*

   Yes! Avoid adding:

   Anyone whose confidentiality you don't trust 100%.

   Also, I do not recommend including your boss, in the beginning, because they evaluate your performance and you need mentors you can be totally open with. After you've built a great relationship with your boss, she or he can become a member on your team. In nearly all cases, you're not going to want to discuss job search with your boss, but they can become a mentor later for other career questions.

   You're building your dream team. You're receiving their support and you're helping them, too. It really is mutually beneficial. Few things will help you in getting hired and navigating your career as much as being part of a thriving career group.

Summary

Step Three: Building your dream team is an imperative for getting hired. Your career team is a trusted circle of people you form to help you best navigate your career, learn, and lean on when you need support, as we all do.

Chapter 5: Build your dream team by drawing from your following resource pools:

- Mentors.
- Career groups.
- Your high school or university alumni groups.
- Professional networking groups.
- Career coaches.
- Friends and family.
- Physical trainers.
- Learning and development outside of work. Take continuing education classes to develop your expertise. Or take classes entirely outside of your core work area to increase your creativity and learn new life skills.

CHAPTER 6: HOW TO CREATE AND RUN YOUR CAREER GROUP

Mark (me for real, not a pseudonym): I was happy with how was developing with individual clients and decided it was time to start meeting with universities. I wanted to talk to them about CareerNav providing coaching to their alumni. There was just one issue. I didn't have many contacts at local universities.

That weekend I went to my career group meeting and asked my half-dozen friends there if any of them had contacts. Immediately a friend said, "A friend of mine is a career center executive at a local graduate school. Do you want me to introduce you two?" I presented to Angela's friend a few weeks later and we're now a coaching option for their alumni.

It's good to have a friend help us in our careers. It's even better to have a group of friends all helping each other.

This experience above is real and I could give you another twenty examples like it. How did they happen? Through the career group I've been a member of in San Francisco for over ten years, which has been one of the most valuable things I've ever done in my career. I highly recommend you create your own.

HERE ARE THE MOST COMMON QUESTIONS I RECEIVE AT ABOUT CREATING A CAREER GROUP

1. *What is a career group?*

It's a small group of five to seven people who meet regularly to discuss all things career. Some of us have full time jobs and come because we want feedback on ideas or challenges at work. Some of us have jobs but are thinking of moving to another company or transitioning to another industry altogether. And some of us are doing a job search and want help with that.

2. *How do you build and run a career group?*

We started our career group when the Internet bubble burst. Our core group all worked in marketing one way or another. We started with about three or four people and our meetings were so valuable our numbers quickly grew.

We meet for about three hours every other month and we've done this fairly consistently for over ten years. In recent years we've had six or seven people at most meetings, so we keep time and give everyone about thirty minutes. We occasionally rotate meetings to different group members' homes, but we have most of them at the home of one member who generously opens her place. As for coordinating schedules, we use Doodle.com to take an online poll of when people can meet.

3. *What are the most important elements to building a successful career group?*

- Fun, positive, group members who are supportive in good times and bad.
- Trust. We are fantastically open about our careers during our meetings. This can only happen when you have 100% trust in your group members. Trust that you won't be judged. Trust that you'll have a receptive audience even if they have to give

challenging feedback. Trust in everyone's confidentiality. In the ten years we've had our group that trust has never been broken.

- Functional and industry expertise. The fact that we have so many people taking three hours out of a weekend day tells you how committed we are. But our members wouldn't be so committed if we all weren't getting so much out of it. That's a testament to our group members because every member has expertise in one area or another.

- Disciplined scheduler. We're fortunate that we have one person in particular who continuously drives the scheduling of our meetings. I doubt we'd meet so often without her efforts.

Here's the list of topics we cover in our career group:

- Resume review/feedback: We email our resumes to our group members to get feedback on how to improve them.

- Linkedin review/feedback: We also get feedback from group members regarding how to improve our Linkedin profiles. See my chapter on how to create a great Linkedin profile.

- Cover letter review: This one is obvious, but I want to highlight the most common mistake, which is writing cover emails that are too long.

- Online job board resources: Job sites have changed a lot in years, so see my section on job sites.

- Networking venues/events: We frequently send each other information regarding interesting meet-ups, industry events, etc. For example, a friend in our career group who was at an industry conference in San Francisco emailed us a link to a summary report called "Digital Trends" that had great information in it.

- Mock interview: This is one of the most valuable things we do as a group. The last time we did this I pretended to be the hiring manager and I interviewed a woman in our group for thirty minutes. Afterwards we gave her feedback on how to improve her answers. She got the job.

- How to answer "Question X": There are just some interview questions that are difficult to answer, so we'll run them by group members for suggestions.

- How to gain new experience: One group member wanted to transition into search engine marketing (SEM), so we connected him with a non-profit where he managed their SEM.

- Sharing contacts or leads with each other: We do this all the time whether it's full-time jobs or part-time projects.

- Identify target companies: If one of our group members describes the type of company they'd like to work at, we often have ideas or make introductions into target companies.

- Share functional expertise: We're constantly learning from each other. For example, one of our group members is an expert in project management, so she walked us through the key steps we need to know.

- Strategic feedback: While maintaining corporate confidentiality, we will lay out strategic crossroads one of us may be at in our company in order to get strategic feedback from the group.

Prioritize search tasks/time management: A job search can feel so overwhelming at times we give each other feedback on what critical next one or two steps to take.

Sticking with it: We support each other emotionally. By providing positive encouragement to each other we help one another stick with it.

Accountability (to ourselves, to each other): Sometimes it's easier to hold yourself accountable to others than to yourself. When I was first developing my website I had a long to-do list. I promised my career group I'd get the site to a certain point by our next meeting. The day before our career meeting I did a number of those to-do's because I didn't want to show up having not fulfilled my promise to them.

Commiserate! Laugh! It's important to the culture of our career group to have fun together. There have been some tears shed during the meetings over the past decade, too, because sometimes people are dealing with very frustrating issues, like job loss.

Whether it's a fun meeting or a bittersweet meeting we always support each other. Also, we often bring food to share. Since we really enjoy spending time together we often go out to dinner after a meeting.

Who are you going to invite to be part of your career group? Who is the first person you want to ask? Why not ask them now? You're building your critical core and now it's time to tap into Step Four and grow your connections.

Summary

Chapter 6. Create your career group of five to seven people with whom you meet regularly. Discuss all things important to your careers such as giving feedback on ideas or challenges at work, career transition and job search.

There are a variety of topics you'll cover in your group including:

- How to navigate your career path.
- How to deal with a boss or colleague who is driving you crazy.
- Job search strategy.
- Mock interviews.
- Resume and Linkedin profile review.

You'll also hold each other accountable, which is valuable. Perhaps more importantly you'll provide emotional support to each other.

Step Four: Grow Your Connections

How to maximize your most powerful resource through relationship building.

Chapter 7: How to Grow Your Connections

Before founding, here's how I've gotten my jobs since I moved to San Francisco in 1998:

AllAdvantage: Job posting by a fellow Kellogg graduate (whom I didn't know) on the Kellogg MBA School's internal jobs site available to students and alumni. He was working at AllAdvantage.

Claria: CraigsList posting by a recruiter.

Shaklee: A good friend of mine from Kellogg was doing a consulting project there and recommended me to the CEO.

Solanova: CraigsList posting by an agency handling the search for the CEO.

CREDO Mobile: An executive recruiter I didn't know contacted me after seeing my Linkedin profile.

Location Labs: An executive recruiter I didn't know contacted me after seeing my Linkedin profile.

Score:
Kellogg connections: 2
CraigsList: 2
Linkedin: 2

Or to look at it more simply:
Connections: 4
CraigsList: 2

Your greatest likelihood of getting your next job is through your connections. Few things in life are as important as connecting with other people and few resources as valuable. There are so many benefits to letting your connections know you're doing a job search: You'll find hidden jobs; a friend or someone you're connected to may recommend you for a job and you may gain the inside track versus an applicant the hiring manager doesn't know.

Even though I "network" more than 95% of the people I know, I don't like the word. I don't view what I do as networking—I sincerely view it as building connections, creating relationships.

I have over 1,200 connections on Linkedin and we help each other out in so many ways. I've made introductions that have led to other people getting jobs. One woman I was coaching was in the negotiation stage for a job she very much wanted but she was uncertain about the total compensation. I remembered I had a contact that worked at the same company. So I introduced them and within two hours she got the full picture of the company, realized certain benefits were particularly generous and that the offer was worth taking. The next morning she finalized her package and is very happy there. And they help me, too, with advice and introductions.

There's a great irony for most people doing a job search: Connecting with others is their best way to find a job and yet networking is what they hate doing the most. Why? Because they feel:

- Awkward about it. This is totally understandable; when you think about it, we're a bunch of strangers coming together to talk for a couple of hours. Some people love meeting strangers, but most feel awkward at first.

- Socially anxious. I was at an industry event one night talking to a woman I'd just met. She's super smart, funny as hell, and we connected immediately. We'd been talking for twenty minutes when she said out of the blue, "If you want to talk to other people I won't mind." I was shocked. I told her I loved talking to her, I was sure I couldn't find anyone as fun to talk to and I asked her why she'd say that. She replied, "I have social anxiety and I feel incredibly uncomfortable meeting new people." I had no idea. I couldn't sense her social anxiety, but I've had friends and colleagues with social anxiety and I know from what they've said that it can feel debilitating.

- Embarrassed. Because they feel as if they're just asking for help. Most of us feel more comfortable helping someone than asking for help.

One coach I was talking to recently works with her clients on developing ice-breakers, because once people manage to start a conversation they're fine. It's the getting started that's difficult. What's your icebreaker?

HERE ARE THE MOST COMMON QUESTIONS I RECEIVE FROM CLIENTS ABOUT BUILDING CONNECTIONS

1. *What are the benefits of growing your connections?*

   I so strongly encourage people to build connections because you'll:

- Find your next job faster. Last week I was coaching someone with his job search. He told me what he was looking for and I happened to know a recruiter who fills executive positions exactly like the one he's looking for, so I gave him that contact. After that meeting, I met with an executive recruiter to interview her for a chapter in this book. She's easily in the top 10% of recruiters in her industry. During our conversation she mentioned she knows another executive recruiter who specializes in exactly the type of job my client is looking for, so I got that recruiter's contact information, too. Within the span of ninety minutes he had two new contacts with targeted recruiters he wouldn't have had if we weren't connected.

- Build connections with people you can rely on for help, support, and contacts. A friend of mine was looking for an introduction to a well-known company and it's one of the few companies where I don't have good connections. So, I emailed my career group and by the end of the day my friend had four new contacts he was able to choose from to get introduced.

- Learn more. If you are applying for a job, do you find there's one part of the job description you wish you had more experience in? You probably have someone you're connected to right now who can teach you that skill. I was at an online company once where we decided it would be a good idea to launch an affiliate network. The only problem was that neither I nor any of my direct reports had ever built or managed an affiliate network. I asked some friends for recommendations and one friend highly recommended a former colleague of hers. I didn't know him, which is why I felt like I had to offer him something for his time. So, I treated him to a very nice dinner at a restaurant of his choice and for two hours he gave me a snapshot of the most important things I needed to know about affiliate networking. I was so impressed by him that I hired him as a consultant and he did two valuable projects for me.

- Get to help people. Sometimes coaches make introductions, but it's more the exception than the norm. But I was coaching an executive once and I made an introduction that led to him getting an amazing job that placed him in a C-suite position.

This was at a large, multinational company, so, obviously, it paid a king's ransom. It felt great to help someone to take their career to its highest level to date.

- Benefit from good karma: As Blanche said in *A Streetcar Named Desire*, "I've always relied on the kindness of strangers." To this day I remember with gratitude all of the people in my life who have helped me in my career, especially those who did it simply because they're kind. How did I become a co-founder of Gumby's Pizza? A friend of mine who was a fraternity brother had an idea to start a restaurant. He asked my roommate, best friend and fellow fraternity brother at the University of Florida to join him because he knew that his father was a successful restaurateur. And then they asked me to join them. Months after that initial idea we opened up our first Gumby's Pizza. Three years after that we had seven stores, at which point I sold out and went back to school. My former partners grew Gumby's Pizza to twenty restaurants nationally, which they continue to run today.

- Make more friends. If I think about my closest friends today, at least a third of them started off "in my network." Meaning, we knew each other but we weren't that close. But with a few, we've built real friendships over time and I no longer view them as in my network—I view them as in my life.

2. *How can I grow my connections?*

Start with the right mindset. Be generous and give without expecting to get. Give because it's the right thing to do. People that only view networking as transactional, meaning I'll only do something for you if you do something for me, turn people off because that's not a relationship. In addition to your alumni and industry organizations, here are some additional organizations you can check out where building connections is core to their mission:

- Meetup events. Meetup.com is "the world's largest network of local groups…more than 9,000 groups get together in local communities each day, each one with the goal of improving themselves or their communities." I've been going to Meetups for years and they're great. You'll find some that are industry specific and others based on interests.

- Chamber of Commerce. Most Chambers are a great resource for professionals. They have events all the time, which are great for building connections. Sometimes I think Chambers are underrated because they've been around for so many decades. But as one executive told me, the two best organizations for building connections in our industry in Northern California are an industry organization we're both active in (NCHRA) and the Chamber.

- NetworkAfterWork.com. Their mission is in their name. They have events in major cities all across America. When a lot of people think of networking they yawn, right? But Network After Work holds its events in "each city's top nightlife destinations." And you have to love an organization that has a martini glass in its logo.

- Young Nonprofits Professional Network: YNPN.org. I love this organization! Do you work for a non-profit or do you want to work for one? Go to YNPN.org to see if they have a chapter in your city—they're in major cities across America. Not only are these people doing amazing work for our society, but they're also having fun building connections.

3. *Why is focusing on shared interests so important in growing your connections?*

Shared interests are awesome for building contacts because we're doing a fun activity together while getting to know each other in a casual way. My most powerful connections come from shared interests: Kellogg, University of Florida (Gators), Anglo-American University, Argentine tango, salsa dancing, Improv classes, soccer, tennis, golf, Prague, former colleagues… Just to take one of these shared interests as an example, here's a few of the awesome people I've met through Argentine tango over the past seven years: NASA scientist, nurse, hand surgeon, fashion executive, owner of a well-known winery, high school teachers, Stanford University professors, filmmakers, students…

At the end of the day, it's better to have a small powerful network of highly influential, well-connected people who want to help you than to have a large network of people you don't know well.

The Do's of Growing Your Connections. Do:

- Understand that you have to give to get. Start with your friends, family, colleagues, universities and your shared interests.
- Use your contacts with great care—don't burn them!
- Read an excellent book on the power of connections, it's called *Grouped* by Paul Adams at Facebook.

The Don'ts of Growing Your Connections. Don't:

- Approach networking only in a transactional way. From my experience over 90% of people follow social norms and don't treat others in just a transactional way. But I had an acquaintance who only called me when he wanted something, so I stopped responding.
- Rush people. Give them time to respond. We're all very busy and often we get requests that we just don't have time to respond to even though we'd like to.
- Ask them for a favor with an "assumptive close" tone. Meaning, don't assume they're going to do you the favor. Literally, as I was editing this chapter I received a message via Linkedin from a guy I had met once to make an introduction for him. The words "please" and "thanks" weren't anywhere in the email—just an assumption that I'll do this for him, which was not the correct assumption.

Now that you've grown your connections, you can use them to find jobs in the hidden job market.

Summary

Step Four: Your greatest likelihood of getting your next job is through your connections. Most people don't like networking because they feel awkward meeting strangers, they may have some social anxiety or they may feel embarrassed due to feeling like they're just asking for help.

Chapter 7: There are many benefits to growing your connections. You'll:

- Find your next job faster.
- Build connections with people you can rely on for help, contacts etc.
- Learn more.
- Get to help people.

There are multiple ways to build your connections including:

- Your alumni and industry organizations. By alumni I mean both university and former colleagues.
- Meetup.com
- Chamber of Commerce.
- NetworkAfterWork.org
- Young Nonprofits Professional Network (YNPN.org).

Chapter 8: How You Can Find the Hidden Job Market

When I was building Gumby's Pizza with my two partners, we hired people all the time without posting those jobs publicly—we hired them because someone at our company recommended a friend of theirs. In every company I've been at since, we've hired people without ever posting those jobs online.

Why? We didn't want to post those jobs online because we'd be drowning in resumes. So we started by asking our colleagues if they could recommend any rock stars. We also asked our trusted network, "Who do you know?"

Welcome to the hidden job market.

Growing your connections is one of the best ways to find the hidden job market. And finding the hidden job market is one of the best ways to get hired.

HERE ARE THE MOST COMMON QUESTIONS I GET ABOUT THE HIDDEN JOB MARKET

1. *What is the hidden job market?*

   The hidden job market are all the jobs that companies haven't posted online yet, or jobs that companies are in the process of creating but haven't finalized yet.

2. *How can someone discover the hidden job market?*

   Some years ago I interviewed at a company and, out of all the candidates, I came in a close second. I didn't get the job then, but I ended the process on the best note possible. I sent letters to the CEO and the President, saying how much I believed in their company mission and that if there were ever an advisory board I could volunteer for I'd love to do that. A little over a year later they decided to create a new position that I had an ideal background for. They never posted this job online. Instead, the CEO contacted me and asked if I wanted the job, which I did. I took it and had a great experience there —and I didn't have to compete against one person to get that job!

3. *So is it pointless to respond to jobs that are posted online?*

I don't want to say that people shouldn't respond to jobs posted online at all, because people get jobs that way very day. I've gotten jobs that way.

But most people are spending their time on the wrong thing. They're spending 80-90% of their time responding to jobs posted online and that's a highly inefficient way to do a job search. That's totally backwards.

I've coached a lot of people over the years who have said to me, "Mark, I'm responding to ten to twenty job postings a day and I'm not getting interviews. Well, the likely reason is they're competing against fifty, one hundred, maybe hundreds of other people that also responded to the same online posting.

So, for the time you do spend responding to job postings online, make sure you're responding to jobs that you truly feel are an excellent match for you. In my job search I did before starting, I only responded to five jobs online and those were the ones where I felt like the job requirement was created for me. I responded to those and three asked me for a phone interview with twenty-four hours, one took a week to respond and the fifth took a few weeks.

4. *If responding to jobs posted online is an unproductive way to get hired, then how come so many companies post jobs there?*

Because it's cheap and easy! To post a job on CraigsList or Linkedin costs less than $200 and within one or two days the company may have hundred of resumes.

It also has the illusion of being easy for companies because it only takes minutes to post these jobs on these sites. But there's a hidden cost to posting jobs online that a lot of companies don't calculate, and that's the time it takes to read through a couple hundred resumes where half of them feel like spam. Spam takes time!

Then you have to reply to all of the applicants, or at least you should, because I have friends to this day that can tell you which companies never gave them the courtesy of a reply—and that hurts the company's brand.

5. *If focusing on responding to jobs posted online is an unproductive way to get hired, then what should I be doing and where should I be going to make sure I am tapping into the hidden job market?*

Connect with people, connect with people, connect with people…

Anyone doing a job search should be spending 80% of their time connecting with people to find the secret job market and the rest of their time responding to jobs online. By connecting with people you'll typically shorten the length of your job search because you'll get the inside track—you may be one of only a very few applicants the company is considering—and in some cases you may be the only person.

6. *How can I connect with people to find the hidden job market?*

Get into the right mindset: "You have to give to get."

Focus on connecting with people where you have shared interests (sports, hiking, cooking, travel, etc.).

Let your entire world know you're doing a search. Most of your friends will help you if they can, but they need to know you're doing a search.

Volunteer. I've met so many great people volunteering. Once I was volunteering at my church and I met a PR expert. We've stayed in touch over the years and helped each other out.

Create a career group, as I detailed in my section on how to create your dream team.

Bottom line: Find your next job before it's posted! It'll shorten the length of your job search and you'll get it with a lot less stress because you'll be competing against only a few people instead of a few hundred people—and you may not be competing against anyone at all.

You're connecting with people to find your hidden job market. If you are a recent college graduate building connections is equally important, as I explain in the next chapter. If you are not a recent college graduate please skip over the next chapter and go straight to Step Five, where I will guide you through mastering your social media.

Summary

Chapter 8. The hidden job market are all the jobs that are out there where companies haven't posted them online yet or jobs that companies are in the process of creating. When you find these hidden jobs you're drastically increasing your likelihood of getting hired.

- Spend most of your time meeting with your connections and going to relevant industry events to find hidden jobs. Spend the minority of your time responding to job postings online.
- Shared interests are an especially effective way to grow your connections because you're doing something you and others both love. Your shared interests allow you to connect with new people based on a friendship first and that goes a lot longer than strictly business.

Chapter 9: The Importance of Mindset and Building Connections for Recent College Graduates

Q&A with Suzi Potts, coach

It wasn't supposed to be like this. Mary graduated in the top 10% of her class from a very good university with a degree in English. She couldn't find a job in publishing after graduation and she had over $80,000 in student loan debt, so she did what we all would've done in that circumstance to pay the bills—she started waitressing. She moved back in with her parents. Her younger brother had moved into her room when she was at university, so she had to move into his old, smaller room (the one with the Spider-Man 3 poster above the bed). Yeah, that was fun (not really). Mary didn't bother redecorating the room because she was only going to be there one or two months until she got her first professional job—three months tops. That was over a year ago. She had interviews during that time, but none worked out.

She was demoralized. But Mary refused to give up, so she kept going to her alumni association meetings.

It was at her next alumni networking event that she met Cathy. Cathy was a HR Director and she was really impressed by Mary. Just as importantly, Cathy's company had an opening and she thought Mary could be an excellent fit for it. Three rounds of interviews and five weeks later, Mary got the job.

It all happened because Mary kept building connections. And in that one moment when she met the HR Director, Mary's life changed.

THE IMPORTANCE OF MINDSET AND BUILDING CONNECTIONS FOR RECENT COLLEGE GRADUATES

Given the Great Recession, millions of students like Mary graduated from universities across America during 2008-2012 and weren't able to immediately get that first entry-level job that so many previous generations had used to launch their professional careers. Instead, millions of college graduates had to take part-time jobs working in areas that have nothing to do with their degrees. Any other generation would have done the same thing. Even though the economy has been recovering, it's still not a strong job market for most recent college graduates.

So, what can graduating seniors and recent college graduates do to gain a competitive edge in getting that first professional job? It all starts with mindset and building connections. It's also critical now for students to get internships while in college because that will help separate you from the crowd upon graduation.

I want to introduce you to an expert in recruiting and developing recent college graduates, Suzi Potts. Suzi is the Director of Recruitment for Southern Wine & Spirits, a multi-billion dollar company, where she leads her company's recruiting efforts at universities. Suzi is also completing her PhD. in Organizational Psychology. And, fortunately for our clients, Suzi is also an expert career coach. I interviewed Suzi to tap into her expertise and here's our Q&A.

1. *What's the mindset of most graduating seniors and recent college graduates you've worked with over the last couple of years?*

   The mindset for the majority of recent college graduates I have partnered with the last few years is grounded in fear and trepidation. I have been in the recruiting and talent management space for the last fifteen years and the biggest difference I have seen is the number of students making a decision to prematurely forego a job search and instead opting to immediately continue their education such as through a Master's program. I believe this decision is driven by the apprehension recent college graduates are feeling given economic conditions, as well as what is perpetuated in the media. However, there are many market-leading organizations that are seeking entry-level talent right out of college. So, if the student becomes overwhelmed by negative information they may overlook the positive opportunities that exist for them. The other big misstep I see relating to mindset is a lack of understanding of the importance of aligning with the student's campus career center. These services are free while attending university and to get this type of support a few years after graduation is quite costly. My key message is that students should capitalize on the resources that are available to them. This requires research and building relationships sooner than your last semester on campus. Those students who are most prepared for a career event or interview are typically those who have participated in networking events as early as their sophomore year.

2. *What kind of mindset do you recommend your clients develop instead?*

The mindset I am recommending for a student is one that is realistic and grounded in the legitimate opportunities that exist. Patience, tenacity, and commitment are important ingredients in the process and will help recent college graduates get hired. Capitalizing on your current connections and building new ones you have not tapped into is valuable. Simple tactical steps that should be taken include asking your friends, professors, and people in your parent's network to help you research certain jobs and industries via informational interviews. Students struggle asking for help and yet they are surrounded by many people who will help if only asked. Successful individuals happy with their career path typically welcome having a conversation with a recent college graduate to help them in their research.

3. *But what about that recent college graduate who has lost confidence because they haven't been able to break through and get that first professional job? What can they do to get going?*

Many recent college graduates lost confidence, so that is quite common. I would immediately suggest connecting with others who have recently graduated as a support system and to build a platform to share your experience and garner insight into what others have done that has been effective. The next step is to introduce yourself to someone who is performing the job that you are interested in learning about and eventually securing. I also recommend some introspection and review of your own value system. In my counseling practice, I refer to them as your "top three deal breaker items." It is imperative for students to know what their three absolute "must have" items are in a job. The deal breaker items are most commonly tied to management style, company mission and culture, opportunity for growth, and team dynamics, and have very little to do with the actual core functions of the position. It took me a lot of time to determine my personal "deal breakers" in a job search because I was so focused on them liking me and wanting me for the role. I often work with students who are extremely enthusiastic about securing a position, but once they land in the role they quickly realize they have overlooked the investigation process during their interviews. A job is ultimately a marriage between your needs, as well as the fit with the mission and culture of the employer you select. While I understand the endgame is to secure the role, if it is not the right match the result will be frustrating and likely just a short-term solution. This can be avoided by clarifying your own individual job seeking needs.

4. *What's the most effective way for graduating seniors and recent graduates to get their first job?*

Students struggle with this question because of their passion and excitement with technology. Technology is a vehicle through which you can navigate your job search and I am a huge advocate of leveraging Linkedin as it offers students an opportunity to share their professional story. However, I see a large percentage of graduating seniors hiding behind technology and using it as their only job-seeking method. This is a misstep since creating a personal connection is the way to set yourself apart and obtain valuable face-to-face meetings. I also see students who do not build their professional network before graduation struggle with the in-person interview process. The key is to strategically develop relationships with people in fields of interest who can educate, introduce, and support you in your goal of securing a full-time job. I still feel personal connections and familiarity with the person performing the hiring function in a company are typically the most effective channels for applicants. The online approach is an abyss of qualified and unqualified people. You are hoping to be in the top group of qualified applicants, but this is a risky proposition. Having a personal connection moves you outside of the unknown and connects you to the decision makers.

5. *What are the most common mistakes people make in connecting with people?*

The most common mistake in networking is to participate out of fear and insecurity. Students are especially concerned that their asking for help will not be well received. I have found the complete opposite to be true, as most successful professionals also had a mentor who took an interest in their career paths and helped them move forward. If you position networking as simply a desire for you to learn about their background, their journey, and any advice they can offer, your inquiry for an informational discussion will almost certainly succeed. Students are afraid of the "no" and thus avoid the sales pitch when asking for help. I suggest using the network of your friends and family as a starting point because you will be more comfortable with them. In addition, preparation for the informational conversation is paramount. A good strategy is to ask a person to coffee or lunch, as this format alleviates pressure. However, you need to come to this conversation with ten to twelve well-crafted questions, which reflect your preparation, enthusiasm, and the importance you are placing on their time.

6. *What are the most important things people need to know about interviewing?*

The key to successful interviewing is grounded in research, preparation, and follow-up. The first component is to know the organization you are meeting with and the individual. I also suggest students clarify the attire in advance with the person calendaring the meeting. Review the company website, Glassdoor, Linkedin, and any other data points that may provide useful information on the organization, and the department or team hosting your meeting. Also, ask the hiring organization in advance the format for your meetings. Is it an individual one-on-one, or will there be panel conversations whereby multiple members of the team are speaking with you simultaneously? I would also inquire about the total number of professionals you will meet with, their respective titles, and the expected length of time for the meetings. The key is to prepare strategic questions, which ensure you can collect the data you need about the position, the management, executive leadership, the corporate vision, culture, and overall business strategy. Interviewing is a skill and those who are effective have practiced significantly. The follow-up can be in an e-mail form, but should also include a handwritten formal thank you note on stationery. Only about 10% of all job seekers follow up with this step, but it will make you memorable—and with the deluge of email today it is much better to receive a piece of mail rather than another email. Make sure you collect all of the business cards of those folks you meet with to expedite this last step.

7. *What are the best qualities Millennials (Gen. Y) bring to companies?*

   In general it's their fresh ideas and viewpoint, which often sees more opportunities than roadblocks when compared to a seasoned business professional. I am drawn to this population's passion, conviction, and willingness to share their thoughts and ideas even when they are not in the mainstream. And certainly their technological competence and comfort level with new ideas is also inspiring and should be leveraged during the interview process.

8. *What are the most common mistakes Millennials make when they join a company?*

Sometimes recent college graduates want to advance too quickly before they've actually mastered the role for which they were hired. There is also a pacing discrepancy as the company may look to reward new hires, but not quite at the pace recent college graduates desire. It is imperative to respect the tradition of the organization while simultaneously suggesting new ideas. The key is to understand the company culture and political landscape where some form of hierarchy drives process. The last point is to set realistic expectations for yourself with your first position. An organization is very different than the educational system you have been accustomed to operating within. There are many who sincerely miss classroom style learning and formal education, but in corporations learning takes place in many different formats and approaches.

9. *When a person gets their first job, what should they focus on to be successful?*

   I would immediately look for a mentor or a more seasoned professional who can help you on your path. Ideally this will not be your manager, but rather someone who is a sounding board to help you sort out questions and concerns, or simply someone with whom to brainstorm. I would hone in on your listening skills and act as a sponge initially to get the lay of the land before moving into fix-it mode unless that was specifically why you were hired. Lastly, I would be authentic and embrace your personality, so that you are going to work in the suit of clothes that reflects your true sense of self. Many students struggle because they want to be perceived as mature and they "act" all day at work. But those who are most successful are ones who can be mature and also authentic.

10. *Any other key lessons you'd like to offer?*

Persistence, tenacity, and a good sense of self will ensure that you get hired for a fulfilling job. The process will be filled with ups and downs, but my experience has been that those who are committed to the process will land where they fit best. If it does not work, and the selection you made is not a good match, then begin the search for your next home. Being happy in your job is a recipe for a happy life.

For recent college graduates I hope you're in a positive mindset. You have tremendous value to offer companies.

It was important in this Step Four that we covered how to grow your connections since that will help you get hired faster. Now we're moving to Step Five so that you can master your social media.

Summary

Chapter 9: Due to the Great Recession recent college graduates have had a highly challenging job market in recent years. The recent college graduates who are getting hired are taking a series of steps that include doing internships while at university, research, preparation, and relentless follow-up.

- Many students underestimate the importance of taking advantage of the resources provided by the school's campus career center.
- Students who are most prepared for a career event and interview are typically those who have participated in network events as early as their sophomore year.
- The informational interview is a gateway to productive conversations.

- Recent college students should connect with others who have recently graduated as a support system and a platform to share your experience.
- The key to successful interviewing is grounded in research, preparation, practice, and follow-up.
- The most desirable qualities that Millennials bring to our market-leading companies are their fresh ideas, viewpoint and technological competence.
- When a person gets their first job they should immediately look for a mentor who can help them on their path.

Step Five: Master Your Social Media

How to create an irresistible Linkedin profile that today's recruiters will notice—everything you need to know.

CHAPTER 10: HOW TO MASTER YOUR SOCIAL MEDIA

I've given up. I just can't keep up with all this social media stuff—I feel like I'm drowning. Do I twitter or tweet? Facebook? How do I figure out my privacy settings? It's just all so confusing. I feel like a digital immigrant surrounded by digital natives.

The social media landscape can be very confusing because there are so many networks out there. I'm going to clarify that confusion by first laying out in this chapter the social media networks you need to know to get hired. Then I'm going to give you an overview of job sites in the next chapter, and then end Step Five by doing a deep dive into how you should be leveraging Linkedin.

It's totally understandable to feel like you have to know all the social media networks out there. But don't worry about them all—just focus on the few that matter most. Unless you need to know a niche social media site for getting hired, just start by making sure you're doing a great job with your profile on Linkedin. I explain how to do that later. If you're already doing a good job on Linkedin, then expand your focus. Here are the four most important social media sites you need to know for getting hired:

- Linkedin: The leading professional networking site, Linkedin is fantastic for inside connections into your target companies, research and personal branding, which is how you market yourself to others.

  Ironically, for all of their laudable expertise in Facebook, Twitter, Tumblr, Pinterest, etc., recent college graduates are behind in this most important career social network. Moreover, college students are missing a huge opportunity by not connecting on Linkedin with their fellow classmates as university freshman. The woman sitting next to you in Introduction to Statistics is going to become a CFO someday. Isn't that someone you want to stay connected with?

- Facebook: Of course most people are already on Facebook and know it well. But people use it primarily in their personal lives. How should you use it professionally? For inside personal connections at your target company (more on that later) and for researching your target company's community. You do this by going to your target company's Facebook page and reading through all of their posts as well as the positive and negative comments by customers. Every company that has an active Facebook page and allows comments will have some negative comments like "I didn't get the product yet that I ordered from your company…" but that's not the point. The most important thing to look for is the company culture that comes through their page and how quickly and effectively the company resolves issues customers bring up on the company Facebook page.

- Glassdoor: A "transparency" job site. Meaning, it makes companies more transparent through the social content posted on their site by employees. Of these four sites that I'm recommending, Glassdoor is the one people typically know the least about.

  How can it help you get hired? Glassdoor provides aggregated job postings, which means it gathers thousands of job postings from a variety of sources for job seekers. Glassdoor gives you salary information, reviews of the company, and photos so you can get a feeling for the culture. Additionally, Glassdoor provides ratings of CEOs that are provided by employees. I'm always recommending that my clients use Glassdoor to read postings about the interview process and typical interview questions. They also have a

Facebook app that allows you to see what friends you have on Facebook who work at your target companies. SimplyHired.com also has a Facebook app that allows you to see current and past companies your friends have worked at.

- Twitter: An extraordinary information network. To this day I hear "I don't get Twitter" or "I could care less that somebody just watched *Here Comes Honey Boo Boo.*" Of course there's banality on Twitter, but there's also massive informational value. When the SEALs took out Osama Bin Laden, a resident in Bin Laden's neighborhood tweeted about the raid as it was happening, not knowing what exactly he was witnessing. Meaning, one of the most top-secret military missions in the history of America was first publicly reported to the world on Twitter as it happened. Ok, that's interesting, but what does Twitter have to do with me getting hired?

For the typical professional today not working in online marketing, Twitter is not as important today to getting hired as the other three social networking sites above. But if you are tweeting regularly and certainly for people working in online marketing, it is important and more so every day. For example, there are companies now that are only posting social media marketing job openings on Twitter.

In a Wall Street Journal article, Jocelyn Lai, a talent acquisition manager for advertising firm GSD&M in Austin, Texas, is quoted as saying she regularly uses Twitter to get a sense of a candidate: "I watch people interact, learn what their positions are, who their best friends on Twitter are, whether they have a sense of humor. From that you can get a pretty good picture."

The WSJ article continues with another excellent point, which is to "re-tweet and converse with hiring managers and employees at companies of interest. If you're currently employed, you can directly message employers *once you have established a rapport.*" Building connections with hiring managers is challenging, but Twitter can be valuable in facilitating online relationship building.

There are two other important ways to use Twitter to get hired:

- Research your target companies. What are the topics they tweet about? What's the tone of their tweets—is it all business? Is it funny? You can tell a lot about a company culture from their tweets. A customer of SEGA's, the video game company, tweeted "what I wouldn't give for @sega to make a new Jet Grind game." The customer's user name was "@HotPikachuSex." SEGA tweeted back, "What I wouldn't give to have not read your user name."

- Build your brand. When used smartly, Twitter can be great for personal branding as proven by Kelly Oxford who sold two TV pilots and published a new book.

  You have to be careful that your tweets don't hurt you—like they often do for sports stars and celebrities. Tweets can positively build a brand or reinforce our perception of a person when Paris Hilton tweets "No, no, I didn't go to England; I went to London."

If you need to scrub your social media profile and take it from the personal to the professional, follow these steps below.

- Photos: I was coaching one recent college graduate and when I saw his Linkedin profile I said, "It looks like you're in a t-shirt at a party holding a beer. Where were you?" He replied, "I was in a t-shirt at a party holding a beer." Feel free to use those photos on Facebook if you have your privacy settings set to "Friends only," but not on Linkedin.

- Comments: I have a friend at a company who, in a moment of frustration, tweeted how executives at a partner company were driving him insane. He realized his tweet looked bad, so he deleted it. And if you're worried about a possible employer screening your Facebook account for inappropriate comments, try a new app called SimpleWash. I used the app and the results didn't show me anything I cared about deleting, but I was surprised to see how often I use the expression "kick butt" or "kick ass"—always referring to one of my favorite sports teams.

- Facebook settings: I do not recommend setting your Facebook page to be viewable by the "Public." If that's your setting, a hiring manager can view all of your photos and comments. Please note that even if you change your Facebook settings from being viewable by the "Public" to only "Friends" that'll only affect your future posts. You may also want to set "Limit Past Posts." Facebook changes its privacy settings with frequency, so check yours often.

- Deleting tweets: The hiring manager at the company you're interviewing at may review your tweets. I'm sure they're full of inspirational pearls of wisdom and not drunken revelries. In case some of the latter slipped through you'll want to delete a tweet like professional athletes and the Kardashians do on a daily basis.

In addition to these four major social sites there are other social media sites that may be important for you, depending on your goal. For example, if your goal is to get hired for a job where micro-blogging is important, you have to know Tumblr. If your goal is to get hired for a design or home decor company, you have to know Pinterest.

You now understand the social media landscape. Next I'll guide you through the major job sites and how they can help you get hired.

Summary

Step Five. Chapter 10: The social media landscape is confusing for many people. Unless you're doing a job search that requires experience with a specific social site such as Pinterest for designers, focus on these four critical social sites:

- Linkedin. This is such a critical social site for professionals I've written a separate chapter about what you need to know.
- Glassdoor. Of the four social sites I'm listing here, Glassdoor is the least known. That's quickly changing.
- Facebook. Assuming they have one, read your target company's Facebook page. You can tell a lot about a company culture by their style and tone.
- Regarding your personal brand, make sure your Facebook page is set to be viewed by "Friends only."
- Twitter. Like a company's Facebook page, read through their Twitter feed to get a better understanding of their culture and customer service. Company tweets are often less filtered, so you can tell more about the company culture.

CHAPTER 11: HOW TO LEVERAGE JOB SITES

Kevin was depressed. "I have trouble getting out of bed in the morning. When I finally get up I sit in my shorts most of the day doing my job search online or playing video games or surfing the Internet. I've been doing my search for months and I'm not getting any responses." I asked him how he was doing his search. "I go to job boards or to company sites, find job postings that are roughly in my area, and then I email in my resume. I normally get an auto-replier saying they've gotten my email, but then I never hear from them again."

The unfortunate thing about Kevin's situation is that it's fairly common. I've personally coached many people in similar states as Kevin and at this moment there are many people across America making the same mistakes as Kevin, making no progress, and ending up demoralized as a result.

The good thing about Kevin's situation is that it's easily correctable. Because so many people have the same experience as Kevin, job boards often get a bad rap. But when used the right way, both job boards and the newer types of job sites can be integral in getting hired.

DEVELOPMENT OF THE JOB SITE MARKET

The job site market is quickly developing. Over ten years ago, millions of dollars started flowing from newspaper print classifieds to job websites. Monster was the first big one and it was quickly followed by others such as CareerBuilder. The big boards were so successful that niche competitors sprang up, like Dice, which focuses on jobs in IT. Today there are thousands of job sites, but most are small, niche players. The big three job sites, Monster, CareerBuilder, and CraigsList, still capture a large part of the revenue in the job site market, but job search tools have been developing quickly and many newer sites have rapidly growing revenues.

Interestingly, these newer sites moved from the job boards' model to a new networking model (i.e. Linkedin) and aggregator model (i.e. Simply Hired).

As a result, there are better tools now for consumers—you don't have to go to multiple individual sites any longer, like Monster or CareerBuilder, because to find most of the job postings relevant to your search there are sites like Simply Hired, Indeed, and Glassdoor that aggregate the postings for you. You can think of aggregator job sites like the aggregator sites we use to buy airplane tickets. Kayak, Travelocity, Expedia, and Orbitz are aggregators, as they compile plane tickets being sold by a variety of individual sites like United, Delta, and many others.

Today's Job Site Market

There are very different job site models now. Some sites are in more than one category like Linkedin. Here's a snapshot:

- Job boards: Monster, Linkedin, CareerBuilder, CraigsList, etc., which are essentially classifieds online. One benefit with job boards is that you can upload your resume for recruiters to find.

- Aggregators: Glassdoor, Simply Hired, Indeed, etc. Aggregator sites have millions of job listings on their sites from thousands of sources, including job sites and listings from companies directly. They include feeds directly from these sources and also "scrape" multiple other sites, which means they scan for new listings and then add them to their site regularly. They show both paid and free listings, like a search engine. As a result, you don't need to go to individual job sites every day because aggregators compile the job postings for you. They use a pay-for-performance model, so the advertiser, which is the company posting the job opening, usually pays-per-click.

- Transparency model. Glassdoor pioneered this model, which is based on giving job seekers a transparent view into target companies through, among other features, anonymous reviews of the company by current and former employees. I love this site!

- Social networking model. Linkedin is the world's leading professional networking site and both Linkedin and Glassdoor are social, meaning they are online communities that interact. In Glassdoor's case, most of the valuable information is employee generated content. When I want to contact a company and I can't think of a friend there, I start by searching through my 1,200 contacts on Linkedin. If I don't find any 1st level connections, I use Glassdoor's Facebook app, which was launched in 2012, to see if I have any friends I'm connected with on Facebook that work at the company. Generally speaking, I'm more reluctant to ask a Facebook friend for a business favor because I mostly separate my Linkedin professional life from my Facebook personal life. But there have been times where I haven't found a 1st level connection via Linkedin and then via Glassdoor's Facebook app I'll find a friend at the company. That's why I marry the two tools together in my searches—it gives me a more complete view into good contacts I have at targeted companies. Oftentimes I have closer contacts on Facebook with whom I'm connected to at a target company than on Linkedin. Simply Hired has both Facebook and Linkedin apps, which allow people to see which companies their Facebook and Linkedin connections work for.

- User-paid job boards: TheLadders, which is a site that caters to people making over $40,000. Companies usually don't pay for a listing there. Users benefit by getting access to higher paying job postings they might not see otherwise. Sometimes these job listings are also available on other job sites.

- Social Applicant Intel: One of the trends I'm seeing in job sites is the further development of social integration points. An intriguing example of this is a new social feature from TheLadders.com, an "online job-matching service." Before I detail the new feature I want to mention that TheLadders is a paid service. They do have a free subscription, but that only lets you preview job titles. The interesting feature they're rolling out to their premium members is what I call Social Applicant Intel. TheLadders describes it this way: "Our new feature *Scout* shows you the compensation, skills, title, work and educational background as well as overall years of experience for each applicant to the jobs posted directly here on TheLadders." Obviously, they're not sharing any personally identifiable information like name or certain job titles.

Even though their names will never be shared, some applicants are going to feel uncomfortable knowing that their compensation range is being shared with the other applicants they're competing against. Personally, though, I think this new feature is valuable for applicants and companies.

For applicants knowing your competitors' compensation, skills, title, work and educational background and years of experience is valuable social applicant intel. As I detail in my Step Eight on out-preparing, doing as much research on the job, your potential boss, and target company is critical to increasing your odds of getting hired. Before this feature from TheLadders it was very difficult to know whom you were competing against. In some jobs I competed for over the past fifteen years, the company I was applying to or the recruiter who made the introduction would give me some non-personally identifiable information about the candidates I was competing against. For example, they'd say, "You have more experience in this area but less in this area." That was valuable for me because it allowed me to position myself against my competitors. If I was interviewing at a medium-sized company and knew a competing applicant had more experience than me, but they had only done strategic work and little execution themselves in recent years, I'd leverage that information during my interview. I'd say, "I'm sure you're interviewing candidates who may have more experience than me, but I'm a roll-up-my sleeves type of person who not only does the strategic work, but also gets the detailed work done, too."

TheLadders' new feature enables applicants to do this type of positioning. This will allow coaches in our group to coach clients applying through TheLadders to analyze the social applicant intel provided. Then we'll work with our clients to best position themselves against their competitors. And for companies, this feature should decrease spam from applicants who shouldn't be applying. Having led numerous searches before, I can tell you that getting resumes from unqualified applicants is a big time-burner for the person in charge of screening resumes. I'd post a job and then have to weed out 80% of the applicants that were wasting the company's time and theirs because they were not even remotely a match. The majority of applicants apply because it's so easy to do and only takes a few minutes. But with this new feature, applicants via TheLadders will quickly be able to see the applicant intel of their competitors. It'll be obvious to people if they're not a potential fit and that should reduce the number of unqualified applicants, which will remove pain and friction from the process for hiring managers and HR.

HERE ARE THE MOST COMMON QUESTIONS I RECEIVE FROM OUR CLIENTS ABOUT JOB SITES

1. *What about using niche job sites?*

   There are thousands of niche job sites and you should find them, too. They may have local listings in your particular job function that the bigger sites don't have. To find these niche sites:

- Search online for the type of job you're looking and add your town or city to the search (i.e., search using the keywords "marketing coordinator, Racine, Wisconsin.")
- Search the local temp agency/staffing/recruiter sites in your area. For example, here in the San Francisco Bay Area there's an outstanding staffing agency called Nelson Staffing. They're in other states, but they're not national yet. They are a leader in local staffing so they can be an excellent source of local jobs. Another leading staffing company is GradStaff, which is headquarted in Minneapolis and has offices in multiple other cities. What's your local version of Nelson Staffing or GradStaff?
- Search the websites of your local industry. For example, here in the Bay Area there's an amazing Human Resources (HR)

organization called the Northern California Human Resources Association (NCHRA). Anyone doing a search for a HR job should join NCHRA, attend their frequent networking events (adult beverages are normally involved in the evening events!), and search their website for local HR listings.

- Search sites of the companies that are on your target list.

2. *How are job sites different today than they were five or ten years ago?*

There's a much better user experience because you don't have to go to every site now. As a result, there's more information that's more easily accessible about job opportunities. Plus, you have sites like Glassdoor that allow you to get more insight than ever before about your target company since employees, past and present, post their reviews of company CEOs and the corporate cultures.

3. *I've heard responding to a job site posting can be like emailing into a black hole? Is that true or do people often get jobs through job sites?*

This is true even for jobs posted on company sites, so this challenge isn't limited to just job sites. The important thing to understand is that most recruiters get so many applicants, most of whom aren't qualified, that they don't have the time to respond personally to everyone. That's why it's so important to apply only to jobs that are a good fit for you, and to customize your response by highlighting your relevant experience and by using targeted keywords in your resume. Otherwise, it's a waste of your time and the company's.

In the past, the paper resume was a screening mechanism. It took job applicants some effort to apply for a job because they had to print a resume, mail it to the company and include a cover letter. People were more selective in applying as a result. What's interesting in this digital age is that for all the benefits online applications have in terms of speed, the big downside is that it's so easy to apply online that people apply for jobs they're not qualified for.

4. *Is networking still the best way to find a job before everyone else?*

Networking is critical, but it's critical to connect with people when they have a job opening. Timing is critical! Unless your skill set is so in demand that they'll create a job for you.

5. *Why should someone in your network help you apply to his company?*

Aside from it being the right thing to do, many companies offer their employees a bonus if someone they recommend gets the job.

6. *What changes do you see coming up in the next one to two years in job sites?*

There are two clear improvements I'm seeing that need to further develop:

- Greater personalization. Job sites are increasingly pushing relevant jobs to you. For example, when I changed my title on Linkedin from "VP of Marketing" to "CEO" I started being shown job postings for CEOs and General Managers. The more Linkedin knows about you the more they can personalize your experience.

- Ongoing social integration points. For example, there's Glassdoor's Facebook app that I spoke about earlier, which shows me Facebook contacts I have in various companies. And for a home design company, wouldn't it be helpful for recruiters if there was a Pinterest app that allowed them to see designers (interior design, kitchens, living rooms etc.) ranked by the most repins as a way to gauge designers who create the most buzz? That would make the recruiter's search process for the hiring of a certain type of designer more efficient. I expect this type of social functionality to accelerate.

3 STEP PROCESS USING JOB SITES TO GET HIRED:

1. Aggregators are a good starting point for everyone. For example, Glassdoor has over twelve million listings. Use niche sites if one exists for your job search (i.e., Dice in tech). Also, set up alerts on all the aggregator sites and a couple of niche sites that best match your search. With alerts you get job listings directly sent to your email inbox, so you don't have to check back into multiple sites daily.

2. Use social networking sites to find out where you have contacts at those companies. This means using every social tool at your disposal: Linkedin, Glassdoor, Facebook, Twitter, Pinterest, Tumblr. Of course you have to work your alumni sites, too, from your university and former companies. Use every angle you can to get a warm connection into a company, so you don't get a cold reception.

3. Use a transparency site like Glassdoor to research before the interview, so you know if you're a cultural fit. If you believe you

are, you'll be better prepared to answer questions in a way that matches their culture. For example, if reviews of your target company describe it as a highly collaborative culture, you'll want to emphasize in your interview how important being a team player is to you.

As you've probably figured out by now, Linkedin is my favorite career site. But Glassdoor is a strong and growing second. It's the one site today that allows you to do all three of these steps I've described above: Aggregate job listings, make connections, and gain a transparent view into companies. If you're now doing an excellent job tapping into all the benefits of Linkedin and Glassdoor you're doing more than the typical professional.

Now that you know the major job sites it's time to do a deep dive into Linkedin, the essential site for most professionals. In spite of the importance of Linkedin, most people have weak, underperforming Linkedin pages. Meaning, their profile is not getting viewed by the hiring managers and recruiters they want to attract. As a result, people are not hearing about great job opportunities. Moreover, it's not positively building their brand. Let's fix that.

Summary

Chapter 11: Job websites have changed drastically in the past decade from essentially being online classifieds to now being incredibly robust. In the beginning Monster.com, CareerBuilder, Hotjobs, and CraigsList dominated the job site space, but that changed as innovative companies like Linkedin.com emerged.

- There are numerous niche sites that exist, so do not limit yourself to just the big sites.

- Aggregator sites like Glassdoor, Simply Hired, Indeed, etc. emerged after the big job sites and they have thousands of job listings on their sites from a variety of sources including the major job sites and company sites.

- Linkedin is the leading social networking site for professionals. It is not only invaluable for professional networking and finding jobs, but also for personal branding.

- The transparency job site model was pioneered by Glassdoor and it gives job seekers a transparent view into target companies via its employee generated content about "anonymous salaries, company reviews and interview questions."

- TheLadders.com is the main user-paid job board and is a site that caters to people making over $40,000. They are launching an intriguing new feature they call "Scout" that will benefit most those willing to out-prepare their competition.

- An effective 3 step process to using job sites includes (a) starting with aggregator sites to find relevant jobs, (b) using social networking sites like Linkedin to find your connections at your target companies, and (c) using a transparency site like Glassdoor to know if you're a cultural fit, get salary information etc.

Chapter 12: How to Create a LinkedIn Profile Page that Recruiters Will Respond To

I was doing my job search and I had a couple of very interesting companies I was in discussion with. Out of the blue I received a message via Linkedin from an executive recruiter who was doing a VP of Marketing search for a leading mobile company here in the Bay Area. She saw my profile on Linkedin, thought I looked potentially like an excellent fit, so she reached out to me. She interviewed me and that went well, so she wanted to forward me to the hiring manager. Just as she was about to do so, she said, "I don't think I have your resume—can you send that over?"

Welcome to the new world of job search.

Linkedin is now the first screening tool many recruiters and companies use even before getting to your resume. Yes, Linkedin is a great social service for connecting professionals and for learning. But it's also a search engine for talent recruiters are seeking. That's why it's so important to make a great first impression on Linkedin—it's one of your key steps to getting hired.

Resumes are still important, but they are not the gating factor they used to be. Oftentimes your Linkedin profile is the first thing a recruiter sees. If they aren't impressed by it they won't ask for your resume. You'll just never hear from them. You may see on your page in the "who's viewed my profile" link that a recruiter viewed your profile. Or you may see "anonymous." Either way, if recruiters are viewing your profile and not contacting you then there can only be one of two explanations: (a) The recruiter was impressed by your profile, but didn't feel your skill set was the right fit, or (b) the recruiter wasn't impressed by your profile. You can't do anything about the first explanation, but you definitely control how much of a "wow" Linkedin profile you have.

Most people we coach today place too much emphasis on their resume and hardly enough on their Linkedin profile. And while there are excellent career centers at many universities across America, there are some that are still letting students graduate without having a Linkedin profile at all! I know because I regularly coach recent college graduates from major universities on how to create their first Linkedin profile. What better time for someone to start building their Linkedin profile than when they're at university making a multitude of friends. Every freshman should have a Linkedin profile because it'll help them get that summer internship. A key step in creating a great profile is to understand what drives results in Linkedin and to understand that you need to know how Linkedin's algorithm works. When I say "algorithm" I mean Linkedin's formula for determining which people or companies show up in your searches and in what order they show up on your results pages.

HOW LINKEDIN'S ALGORITHM WORKS: A STATE SECRET

I have to start with a confession: I have no idea exactly how Linkedin's algorithm actually works. The formula they've created that determines our search results is a closely guarded, proprietary secret. In fact, most people who work at Linkedin don't know the exact weighting of the various elements of their algorithm. Just to give you an example of how complicated algorithms can be, most search experts say there are well over one hundred factors in Google's search algorithm. What's more, both Google and Linkedin are frequently changing their algorithms. I see that often in how I get better, more relevant search results over time on Linkedin.

Nevertheless, even though we don't know exactly how Linkedin's algorithm works, there are clearly best practices we do know about. We know what Linkedin has told us and we know what we can prove through testing. Meaning, I've done multiple tests where I'll just make one change to my profile, i.e., adding targeted keywords, and then measure the increase in "views" I get.

Before I jump into the details, let me give you this simple summary: What is important to Linkedin's algorithm today is (a) how many people you're directly connected to and (b) how frequently you repeat targeted keywords throughout your profile. Some people will emphasize the importance of shared groups or other factors, but these are the two factors you should focus on initially. Please keep in mind Linkedin is frequently changing their algorithm, which is why it's important to stay current.

I go into more detail later, but the most important first step to take to increase the ranking of your Linkedin profile in search results for targeted keywords is this: Complete your profile! I know this sounds obvious, but too many people haven't done this core first step. Linkedin has told us that a completed profile gets ranked higher. Specifically, you need:

- Headline with targeted keywords. Your headline is immediately underneath your name, and it's critical to have a compelling one. I explain how to do that later, but be sure to include one to two of your most important targeted keywords in it.

- Summary with targeted keywords. Your summary is underneath your top section under the "Background" heading. Along with your headline this is also a critical component.

- List all jobs and descriptions you've had with targeted keywords.

- Add a photo. It needs to look professional. Make sure it's not a party photo you'd use on Facebook.
- Include your education, postal code, and industry.
- Fifty or more connections. Start with your friends and family. Invite your past and present colleagues. If you're a graduating student or recent college graduate, invite your classmates.
- At least five skills. You can list up to fifty.

To get feedback from Linkedin about how to strengthen your profile, login to your account and use their online tool. Linkedin will display on the right side of your profile improvements that can be made.

Now that you've completed your profile, let's do a deeper dive. Linkedin's algorithm rewards the following factors:

Networks of Connected People

There is tremendous value in you having 1st level connections. While I always discourage spamming people, you should be connecting with everyone you have a legitimate connection with. Of the 1,200 people I'm connected to today I probably don't remember meeting at least 10% of them, but we connected to each other earnestly. By creating as many authentic first level connections as possible you're creating your own search engine for your professional life. The more 1st level connections you have the more powerful your search results because you'll not only have them show up in your results, but their connections will show up, too.

This is why trust is so critical. I'm often looking for an expert for my business or for a friend. When I do a search in Linkedin, I frequently don't see a 1st level connection that has the specific expertise I'm searching for, but I'll see some 2nd level connections that do. So, I contact my 1st level connection, who is connected directly to that person, and ask him to evaluate the person's level of expertise. I trust a friend's opinion of a potential vendor more than I trust the vendor's website.

Keyword-focused Content

Currently keywords are critical in driving search results. In Search Engine Optimization (SEO) it's called "keyword density," which means you want to use your targeted keywords repeatedly, but in a natural way in order to increase your rankings in search results. This is what companies do every day on their websites to increase their rankings in Google. The same applies with Linkedin, but there's a key difference today. Years ago people could game Google's algorithm by doing "keyword stuffing" in order to come up higher in search results. Those days are over since Google strengthened its algorithm and today sites are punished in the rankings if they're trying to game the system. As much as I love Linkedin, their algorithm needs to be improved because it's still possible to game their system and people do. I think keyword stuffing is terrible for personal branding and I never recommend it, but you need to know it exists. Please be sure to use targeted keywords in a natural way. I expect that Linkedin will improve its algorithm so that it starts punishing keyword stufffers by dropping them in search results or banning them altogether. I hope that'll happen sooner than later in order to create better search results for us all.

To see an example of what I mean by keyword stuffing, do a search for people on Linkedin using keywords like "coach." Typically what will happen is that your top results will include some of your 1st level connections that have expertise in that area and some of your results will include some of your second level connections who are in shared groups with you. But you'll probably also have some people in your results who are keyword stuffing. Take a look at their profile to see what I mean. Do they use the "coach" keyword naturally throughout their profile? If so, kudos to them. Or are they gaming the system? I just did a search on Linkedin for the keyword "coach" and the person who came up first in my results stuffed the keyword in his profile over 100 times. Yes, 100. He has little coaching experience, but just by repeating "coach" ad nauseam throughout his profile he's degrading the quality of my search results.

Another important point regarding keywords is to fill out your experience with content from every one of your jobs. A very common mistake is to just list your previous companies and titles. This is not enough. To increase your ranking in search results you need to fully build out your page and list the core content under each title on your resume to your profile.

I'm intentionally listing this keyword-focused content bullet above Linkedin Groups because even though both are important, I've seen bigger increases in search results from adding keyword-focused content under every company than I've seen from only joining more groups.

Linkedin Groups

This is another factor that drives search results, so join as many relevant groups as you like. One or two is not enough. Most groups I've joined act professionally and don't spam. If you're particularly worried about this, please don't be, because after you join you can change your settings so that you don't receive any emails from them. To do so, login to Linkedin and go to your "Settings" page.

Once there, click on the "Groups, Companies & Applications" tab. From there click on the "Set the Frequency of Group Digest Emails" link. That'll allow you to set any group to "No email" if that's your preference.

What Linkedin's New "Skills & Expertise" Feature Means for You

Last year Linkedin launched a new "Skills & Expertise" feature and that's created a lot of buzz. It makes a lot of strategic sense because now we can give and receive one-click endorsements. Integrating this social feature into endorsements should also have a real payoff in terms of making Linkedin's algorithm more robust, which means we should all get more relevant search results over time and that's great. Once we get there.

Linkedin's algorithm isn't there yet and there have been some unintended consequences along the way. The way the algorithm seems to work is that if a number of your contacts endorse you for a specific "Skill & Expertise" then that skill is more likely to be presented to your other contacts for endorsement. This is great if you like the "Skill & Expertise" you were endorsed for, but not if you don't. For example, my skill in "email marketing" has been endorsed by multiple friends from tango, salsa dancing, Improv classes, a woman from church, and a number of childhood friends, none of whom I've ever worked with! Curiously enough, Linkedin's very logical strategic goal of creating a better algorithm while adding the simplicity of one-click endorsements has actually created more work for me. I've literally had to ask colleagues I've worked with to endorse me for any "Skill & Expertise" other than "email marketing." So, Linkedin has to work out some of the kinks with this feature and I'm assuming they're doing exactly that. For example, could this feature be limited to people you've actually worked with? In the meantime, I suggest that you choose the three to five most important areas of "Skill & Expertise" and ask your colleagues, past or present, who truly know your experience to endorse you. That'll make those "Skill & Expertise" areas offered more frequently for endorsement to your other contacts.

If you don't want your Endorsements displayed, you can always hide them. Likewise, you can add or remove certain Endorsements.

GET FEEDBACK ON YOUR CURRENT PROFILE

Before you start improving your Linkedin profile you need to understand how others perceive your page. This feedback can be difficult to hear, but it's important. Ask three or four trusted people and, ideally, any recruiter friends you have to quickly read your Linkedin profile and then email you their answers to these questions:

- What do you think my goal is with my profile? For example, is it to "find an engineering job in a large company," "build my personal brand as an expert in management consulting," "build my company's brand as the first HR vendor to offer consulting for this aspect of Obamacare?"
- What are my greatest areas of expertise?
- How would you describe my personal brand in one or two sentences?
- Does my profile clearly communicate what you think my brand is? If not, why not?
- Imagine that I'm doing a job search and you're the hiring manager. Now imagine that you have a job opening at your company for the type of job I'm seeking and that I have the

skill set to get the job. On a scale of 1-7 (1 being "Definitely would not hire" and 7 being "Definitely would hire"), how would you score your likelihood of hiring me based solely on the impression my Linkedin profile makes?

- If you scored less than a 7, how can I improve my profile?
- Any other suggestions?

When I'm coaching people they almost always get feedback that surprises them. It becomes clear to them that people are not viewing their profiles the same way they are. I'm friends with one of the country's best direct response copywriters and he likes to say, "I don't know what I've written until someone tells me."

Turn Off Activity Alerts Before You Start Making Changes to Your Profile

Many people we coach who are thinking about starting a search are understandably nervous that their boss or someone at their company might see multiple updates in their profile and figure out they're doing a job search. For example, their boss might see that they've updated their experience in their profile, connected with three new recruiters, joined two new job search groups, and started following new companies. I recently saw a former colleague's updates in my feed and I immediately thought to myself, "It looks like he's doing a job search."

If you're in this boat don't worry about it, just turn off your "Activity Alerts." This will allow you to make updates to your profile without them being broadcast. To make this change go to "Settings," then in your "Profile" tab click on the "Turn On/Off Your Activity Broadcasts." On the next screen you'll be able to turn them off.

Now you should be ready to write a great Linkedin profile. Here's my method for how you can do it. Answer these questions:

- What is your goal?

  You have to be clear on what you're trying to achieve with your Linkedin profile before you can improve it. Are you trying to get a job as a financial manager? A VP of HR? An entry-level position in accounting? Do you want to change careers and use your transferrable skills to get that new job? Are you trying to build your brand as an expert in social media?

- Who is your target?

  Are you trying to get recruiters to contact you? What kind of recruiters? Marketing? Finance? Tech? Are you about to email an HR manager at a target company? If you have your own business, do you want to impress your targeted companies when they check out your website and Linkedin profile?

  To Do: Describe your target audience. Here's an example of what that could look like: "Hiring managers and/or recruiters for an online marketing manager position in a consumer tech startup in the Austin, Texas area."

- What keywords are most important to you?

  An area of expertise for me is online marketing, so, as an example, here are some keywords important for that kind of profile: Online marketing, Internet marketing, online customer acquisition, social media, SEM, SEO, affiliate marketing, email marketing, increasing online conversion rates, web analytics...

To Do: Identify the keywords most important to you and then use them naturally throughout your Headline, Summary Statement, and Experience.

- Thinking about your goal, your target audience, and your most important keywords, write the most compelling "Professional headline" you can for your profile. For example: "Experienced online marketing manager with expertise in doubling customer acquisition and increasing retention rates by 28%."

- What "wow" achievements do you have that are relevant to supporting your headline? For example, were you a Top 10% producer, chosen by the CEO or your boss to lead an important project, or have you founded a company before that achieved X?

  To Do: List your "wow" achievements in your Summary Statement.

  Examples:

  "Increased online revenue by 65% in 3 months by launching retargeting campaign."

  "Increased retention rate by 28% in 2 months."

  "Chosen by CEO to present at South by Southwest"

- What are your two or three areas of expertise?

  Meaning, what is your "unique value proposition" or your "point of differentiation" in comparison to your peers?

  Example: Online marketing acquisition, building online communities, mobile marketing, etc.

  To Do: Add your points of specific expertise into your Summary Statement and then expand on them in your Experience section underneath it.

- Don't be too modest. Don't be arrogant, but this is not the place to hide your skills.
- Add Recommendations. They are important and many people really do read them. Yes, a lot of people discount them because they view recommendations as something friends do for each other. This is true, but there's insight in them, too, if you look for the details. One executive I've coached said she reads every single recommendation and focuses on expertise and tone. Meaning, does the recommender talk what a nice person Joe is, but not talk about specific areas of Joe's expertise? And regarding tone, this executive is certain she's able to suss out half-hearted recommendations like "Joe's a nice guy who..." versus the high performers like "Joe inspires his teammates." Lastly, ask yourself if the recommendation feels authentic. I've read many that feel like a badly written corporate press release—dry and boring. In such cases, I assume the person emailed their recommender language to use and that never feels real.
- Remember: Recruiters don't read Linkedin profiles, they scan them. You only have a few seconds to make a great first impression.

LINKEDIN'S PREMIUM ACCOUNT

I'm often asked by people if they should upgrade to a paid business account, and even though I'm a Linkedin evangelist, in most cases I don't think it's necessary. But the one time it could be worthwhile is when you're doing a job search and you're seeing specific hiring managers and/or recruiters you want to contact with whom you have no other connection. If that's the case, it can be worth subscribing for a couple of months because you'll be able to send an "inMail" directly to those people even if you're not connected to them. Linkedin's Business account costs $25 a month when paid monthly. You get a number of benefits from this paid subscription, but for me the most important ones are:

- Three inMails. An inMail allows you to send a direct message to anyone on Linkedin. With a free account you can message all of your 1st level connections, but not your 2nd or 3rd level connections. This is where an inMail can be so handy. If you have a free Linkedin account you'll have to purchase inMails at $10 per inMail. With the Business subscription you get three inMails per month. If you've recently started a job search it may be a better idea for you to not subscribe immediately and see how many inMails you purchase in the first month. If you purchase three inMails and you expect that to continue for four to six months then it's probably worth it for you to switch to the Business subscription for that short period. You'll be paying the same amount but with the subscription you'll get, among other things, more introductions, be able to see full profiles of 3rd degree and group connections, and you'll have more advanced search filters.

- Fifteen introductions versus five with Basic. Much like inMails, I normally find introductions valuable just to people doing a hardcore job search. I'm a power Linkedin user and I haven't had the need for more than the five introductions that come with the free account. But if you're doing a power search and you're finding yourself sending a lot of introduction requests then you very well may need more.

- See full profiles of 3rd degree and group connections instead of just 2nd degree. If you're doing a job search now this can be useful when you want to research people you're interviewing with. If you have at least one 1st level connection at the company there's a good chance that connection will be a 1st level connection with these other people. If so, you'll be able to view their full profiles because they're 2nd level connections of yours. But if you don't have any connections in the company, or any other 1st level connections to the people interviewing you, then being able to fully view 3rd level connections can be valuable and worth upgrading for.

- More search results and advanced search filters. With a free account you get 100 search results and with a Business account you get 300.

You've created a great Linkedin page. You're starting to get more relevant recruiters viewing your page. Now it's time to get introductions to hiring managers for potential jobs you feel are a bull's eye fit.

GET INTRODUCED TO HIRING MANAGERS THROUGH YOUR LINKEDIN CONNECTIONS

I don't have that many contacts.

My network is really small—-it can't help me find a job.

People don't want me asking them to help me with my job search.

I've heard every concern above. They're all valid and they all feel real. With virtually every person I've coached they turn out to be perception and not reality. You have more powerful connections than you realize. You also have more connections than you realize who will gladly help you as soon as you ask them. It's important to spend time on creating your excellent profile because now I'm going to guide you through how to ask a contact of yours to make an introduction for you. You only get one chance to make a great impression on the person you're going to be introduced to. Assuming you've already done the work in creating a great Linkedin profile you're ready to move forward. Here are the steps you should take to tap into your connections to get introduced to hiring managers, recruiters, and other connections who can help you get hired.

1. **Send out your invitations to connect.**

   Send them to your friends, family members, current and past colleagues, and your parents' friends you personally know. This is not a time to be embarrassed about using family connections—this is what friends are for.

2. **Create your short list of people you'd like to be introduced to.**

   After your contacts accept your requests, they'll be 1st level connections to you. You'll then be able to go through all of their 1st level contacts, which is what you do to come up with a short list of companies/people/positions that are most interesting to you.

3. **Send out your introduction requests.**
   Send them to your 1st level contacts via Linkedin, asking them to forward your introductions to their 1st level contacts. In these requests, ask for informational interviews, or if you've seen an opening at their company ask if you can talk to them about the company culture, or make an introduction for you to the hiring manager. Only ask to be introduced to people who are an excellent fit for your search—don't ask for favors from someone you don't know if the job doesn't truly excite you.

Assuming your 1st level connection feels comfortable doing so, they'll forward your introduction request to their 1st level contact (a 2nd level contact to you). Hopefully that introduction request will be accepted. If it is you have started a conversation with someone who can hopefully help you with your job search.

You've created a great Linkedin page that recruiters will respond to and that will strengthen your brand. Certainly you want to spend most of your time meeting with your personal connections to find opportunities, but you also want to partner with recruiters. You want to take Step Six and build long-term partnerships with the best recruiters in your space so you can turn them into your career agents.

Summary

Chapter 12: Linkedin is a massively valuable social networking site for professionals.

- How Linkedin's algorithm works is a state secret. There are a variety of factors that increase your ranking in search results, but the most important one to start with is to be sure that you complete your profile.
- After you've completed your profile, the three main factors that will increase your rankings in search results are keyword-focused content, being in networks of connected people, and Linkedin groups.

- Linkedin's new "Skills & Expertise" feature is strategically wise because it enables one-click endorsements. However, there have been some unintended consequences that you want to manage.
- Getting feedback on your current profile is important. Before you start improving your Linkedin profile you need to understand how others perceive your current page.
- Turn off activity alerts before you start making changes to your profile.
- One of the most valuable features of Linkedin is the ability to get introduced to hiring managers through your 1st level connections.

Step Six: Partner with Recruiters and Staffing Agencies

Ever wish you had an agent to help build your career and maximize your compensation? Here's how to get one for free.

Chapter 13: How to Turn a Recruiter into Your Career Agent

There is not an agent in baseball more prepared for contract negotiations. He will demonstrate how each player is so special that he has to be considered different than the market place. There will be the day that Scott Boras becomes the first agent inducted into the National Baseball Hall of Fame.

Jim Bowdon, ESPN.com

"Drew treats us like family—we know he's loyal. He offers no apologies; he is determined to fight for his clients."

Client speaking about NFL football agent, Drew Rosenhaus

Professional baseball and football players have super agents like Scott Boras and Drew Rosenhaus fighting for them when they sign with a team. Agents are often controversial, but they will go to extraordinary lengths, night and day, to help professional athletes (and actors, singers, authors…) make the next best career move while negotiating the best contract possible.

Imagine if you had an agent like Boras or Rosenhaus fighting for your career success. I'm not suggesting you find one recruiter to work with exclusively—that wouldn't make sense. I'm also not suggesting that a recruiter contractually become your career agent, but I am saying you have a mindset where you view your three or four best recruiters as your virtual career agents. I've worked with a couple of exceptional recruiters for years and they don't even know I view them as my career agent. That's how much focus and attention I give them when appropriate. If you do this your virtual career agents will place you in valuable jobs over the course of your career.

They won't view you as a transaction; they'll view you as a trusted partner.

How can you do this? I want to lay out the recruiting landscape first and then I'll explain how to take your relationship with your recruiter to a higher level.

HERE ARE THE MOST COMMON RECRUITER QUESTIONS I RECEIVE FROM OUR CLIENTS

1. 1. *What is a recruiter? Is a recruiter the same thing as a headhunter?*

   A recruiter is someone who recruits for companies to fill their full-time jobs for them. And, yes, recruiters are often called "headhunters." Some recruiters are internal at the company and some are external. Companies use external recruiters when they don't have the time or expertise to manage the search themselves. External recruiters view internal HR recruiters as "competition" in a sense, because HR may fill the role before the recruiter. But often this does not happen because internal recruiters may be focused on filling forty positions and can't give the attention to one search that an external recruiter can.

2. *What's the difference between a recruiter, a staffing agency, and a temp agency?*

   Typically, a staffing agency recruits for both short-term and full-time roles. Temp agencies are different because they typically hire for roles that aren't permanent.

3. *What are the different ways recruiters find candidates?*

- Referrals from someone in their network. Their relationships drive their success.

- Linkedin: Leading recruiters have massive amounts of contacts in their personal database and on Linkedin. If they can't find enough excellent candidates from their personal network they'll search Linkedin and contact the professionals that impress them the most.

4. *When I see a job posting from a recruiter that I am perfect for, what should I do next to get an interview?*

   Use your network!

- Do you know the recruiter?

- If not, use your network (Linkedin, Glassdoor, your alumni association...) to see if you can get an introduction to the recruiter.

- If you don't have any connections to the recruiter, call them by phone.
  The last thing you want to do is email the recruiter blindly. But if you have to, focus on your skills relevant to the job posting and your passion for the job and company.
  One leading staffing agency here in the San Francisco Bay Area only invites in 10% of the people it hears from, so these steps above are important.

5. *How can I pass the recruiter screening to get an interview with a company?*

Preparation, preparation, preparation. In Step Seven I explain how to out-prepare, so I cover those details there. But remember—to impress the recruiter when you first contact them go the extra mile in your preparation. To do that you want to:

- Review the recruiter's Linkedin profile beforehand so you can talk about common interests you share: Companies, university, travel, etc.
- Highlight why your skill set is an excellent match for the job.
- Highlight why you're a great cultural fit. Also, when you talk to the recruiter ask them to give you any additional information they have about the culture.
- Communicate how excited you are about this possibility!
- The most important thing is to build the best relationship you can with the recruiter. Even if you don't get this job, the recruiter may have one for you in the future.

6. *Assuming I make it past my screening call with the recruiter, what should I do when I interview with the company?*

You want to achieve the same goals that you have when interviewing with the recruiter. Impress the company through your preparation. The more you prepare the more you'll learn if you truly feel like you're a fit with the company culture, their mission, and your future boss.

Additionally, you have these goals:

- Review the Linkedin profile of everyone that'll be interviewing you beforehand so you can talk about common interests you share.

- Build the best relationship you can with the hiring manager and everyone else you meet.
- Send handwritten "thank you" cards afterwards.

7. *What's the difference between a contingency and a retained recruiter?*

   A contingency recruiter only gets paid by the company if a candidate they present to the company gets hired. So, contingency recruiters may be competing against multiple other recruiters and the company's internal HR team, too, to fill the position.

   A retained recruiter, conversely, has exclusive rights to fill the position and gets paid by the company whether the company ends up filling the position with an internal candidate or an external candidate found by the recruiter.

8. *Who pays the recruiter if a recruiter helps me get a job?*

The company pays.

HOW TO FIND EXCELLENT RECRUITERS

The best way to identify the best recruiters in your industry is to ask your connections who the best recruiters are that they've worked with. Then when you meet with a new recruiter remember that you're screening them as much as they're screening you. Here are important questions to clarify with the recruiter:

- What types of positions and companies do they do searches for?

- Do they typically do retained or contingency searches?

- Will they maintain your confidentiality? Unless you've given a recruiter permission to introduce you to a specific company, you do not want recruiters telling others that you're doing a search because that might get back to your current company.

- Make sure the recruiter never presents your resume without your permission. One woman I was coaching was doing a search and a recruiter contacted her about an opportunity. The recruiter asked for her resume to get to know her better and then, without her permission, sent her resume to the company. She started doing research on the company culture and decided she wasn't interested in it. It turned out the company wanted to talk to her and she had to say no, which created an awkward situation. Needless to say, she stopped working with that recruiter.

- The other reason it's important that a recruiter not present you to a company without your permission is that, if you're working with two recruiters, you want to be sure both recruiters aren't presenting you at the same time. That just looks bad for everyone.

Because recruiters are so important I interviewed a leading executive recruiter and asked her what the most important qualities she looks for when reviewing Linkedin profiles and resumes. This executive recruiter said she looks for the following:

- Skill set that shows you have the relevant, excellent experience.

- Quality of the companies you've worked for. Here in the innovation capital of the world, new startups appear at the speed of light. And yet there is still clearly a cache that comes with having worked for large iconic brands. If a recruiter is doing a search for a client who wants candidates who have world-class design experience, all things being equal, the recruiter is going to put the designer from Apple at the top of their list over designers who have experience at good, but not great design firms.

- History of success that clearly communicates your personal achievements at your company. People often make the mistake of listing corporate achievements like, "Revenue for my division grew 40%" when they actually had little or nothing to do with that growth. Instead, if you're the email marketing manager for your division, make statements about results you controlled like "increased email marketing conversion rates by 22%."

- Progression of promotions in every company you've been at. Recruiters want to see that if you started as an entry-level coordinator at Company X that you were promoted to manager level within a couple of years, then senior manager, director…

- Stability. My Grandfather worked as a crane operator at General Electric for over forty years. One career, one job, one company. Those days are long over, obviously, as people today often work at four, five, and six companies during their career. But recruiters still want to see some stability and it's a red flag if a candidate has been consistently jumping companies every other year.

My interview with the executive recruiter continued and she said that if she's impressed by the candidate's Linkedin profile and resume that she'll then interview the candidate over the phone. Here are the most important qualities she's looking for during interviews:

- Cultural fit: Are you super competitive? If so, you probably won't fit in a highly collaborative culture. Is having a flexible work schedule important to you so you can come and go as long as you hit your objectives? If so, you probably won't fit into a highly structured 9am-6pm company where it's frowned upon if you arrive past 9am or leave early even if you are getting back online in the evening.

- Strategic thinking: Are you able to connect the dots and give your boss and other executives recommendations regarding what you believe the company's strategy should be?

- Communication skills: You're going to need to influence colleagues, so are you clearly and compellingly able to make your point?

- Presentation skills: While not used regularly in every job, presenting well is critical in most functions like marketing, sales, HR, and finance.

So, the recruiter contacts you and you impress them. Great. Here's the one question that can trip you up: "Why would you be open to leaving your company?" The worst answer is "for more money." If more money is your only motivation, how long are you going to be at the next company before jumping to another company again for more money? That would make the recruiter look very bad to their client and you can kiss goodbye any chances of building a long-term relationship with the recruiter. Instead, if you want to become a sales director, you could say, "in order to become a sales director I'd leave for an opportunity that would give me a bigger opportunity to develop in this area in order to have a more strategic and less administrative role.

HOW TO TURN A RECRUITER INTO YOUR VIRTUAL CAREER AGENT

Recruiters are like every other professional group: There are good ones, poor ones, and average ones. But the best ones you want to build relationships with are the great ones—the best of the best. I'm talking about the top 10% of those recruiters that simply operate at a higher level and have more interesting opportunities. They also understand their candidates' strengths and weaknesses better, which allows them to know if a company is truly an excellent fit for a candidate or not.

Let me give you an example. Having worked in San Francisco in online marketing for the past fifteen years, I've met over one hundred marketing recruiters—both individuals and agencies. Most of them are in the Bay Area, but I've also talked to recruiters in other states and even in London. Out of all of them, there are about a half dozen that are elite and I've built partnerships with three of them. Here's how I did that with a one of the best recruiters in the industry.

Paul is an independent executive recruiter and highly connected. I met him years ago and we've regularly stayed in touch since. One time, as a favor to him, he asked me if I'd meet with one of his clients, a co-founder of a funded company, to give him a snapshot of online marketing strategies. I met with the co-founder for hours. That was so helpful for him he asked if I'd meet with his three partners. I did that over a long dinner. It was very helpful for these entrepreneurs and it further strengthened my relationship with the recruiter, so I was happy to do it. This transformed my relationship with this executive recruiter from a transactional one to a partnership.

Do's:

Here are the top 3 things you can do for a recruiter to transform them into your career agent:

1. **Always return their calls.** Understand and value the unique, important work they do, such as having expertise to know which companies and jobs you're best suited for. Plus, the best recruiters have strong relationships with companies and they can introduce you for jobs you wouldn't know of otherwise. Even if you did know about the opening, your strongest entry point may be through an outstanding recruiter.

2. **Even if you're not interested in the job, try to send them an excellent referral.**

3. **Stay in touch on a regular basis even when you're not looking.** This is not a transactional relationship—you're building a long-term partnership.

Final Point:

After a recruiter has placed you in a company, of course the most important thing is to do a fantastic job for your new company. By delivering as much value as you can at your new company you'll make your recruiter look great and be on your way to transforming your recruiter into one of your virtual career agents.

Take care of your career agents and they'll take care of you. But staffing agencies can also play an important role and I want to walk you through how they work, and what you need to do to impress them so they help you get hired.

Summary

Step Six. Chapter 13: Imagine if you had a super-agent fighting for your career success. Develop a mindset where you view your three or four best recruiters as your virtual career agents.

- If you see an opening you're interested in from a recruiter you don't know, the best way to get introduced to them is via referrals from someone in your network.
- For most professionals Linkedin is essential to their career because if a recruiter can't find enough excellent candidates from their personal network they'll search Linkedin.
- Assuming you have the skill set for the job opportunity you're responding to, preparation is the most important thing you need to pass the recruiter screening.
- The most important qualities recruiters are looking for when screening your Linkedin profile or resume are skill set, a history of success, the quality of the companies you've worked at, a progression of promotions or increasing responsibility, and stability.
- When a recruiter is interviewing you, in addition to the qualities in the bullet above, they are evaluating your cultural fit, strategic thinking, and communication and presentation skills.
- To build relationships with recruiters over time always return their calls and emails, send them excellent referrals even if you're not interested in an opening they've emailed you, and stay in touch with them on a regular basis.

Chapter 14: How to Partner with a Staffing Agency

Henry was having trouble finding a full time job and he was losing his motivation. So, to make some money and to stay busy he started temping. One of his temp jobs was with a healthcare organization where he was working in technology. Based on the experience he got temping, he ended up getting a full time job at a biotech company. He ended up staying at that biotech company for over a decade where he had a very successful career—until he was recruited for a more fulfilling role at another leading company at a higher salary. It all started because of that three-day assignment he got through the staffing agency.

Venture capital-funded startups, executive recruiters, dream teams, social media, career agents… they all sound sexy. What often gets overlook in this market is staffing agencies. And that's a mistake—staffing agencies can play a critical role in getting hired, but they're often not well understood. Next I will explain the most important things you need to know about staffing agencies.

HERE ARE THE MOST COMMON STAFFING AGENCY QUESTIONS I RECEIVE FROM OUR CLIENTS

1. *What is a staffing agency? Is it the same thing as a temp agency?*

   It's an agency that companies hire to fill jobs for them. Staffing agencies can be focused on temporary contract or permanent roles. Their temporary roles are typically part-time jobs that can last anywhere from one day to months. And in some cases they can be full time, which is how a staffing agency is different from a temp agency. A temp agency is focused on filling temporary jobs, not full time.

2. *Is there a way I can find out about jobs at staffing agencies before everyone else to increase my odds of getting one?*

   Yes, by building the best relationship possible with the recruiter, even if you don't get the first job you apply for. You'll increase your chances of finding the hidden job market if a recruiter is impressed by you because they'll contact you first when a new job opens up that's a fit for you.

3. *How do I turn a short-term assignment into a full-time job?*

   Temporary jobs often turn into full-time jobs, so even if you only have a two-day assignment, treat it seriously and over deliver. Focus on:

   Being as productive as possible. If the boss asks for research to be done in three hours, deliver it in two.

   Building the best relationships you can with the people at the company. We all want to be surrounded by people at work that we like, so build connections as quickly as you can during your assignment.

   Being on time! I know this sounds obvious, but many people aren't on time and that doesn't look good to the company.

   Not spending time on personal things at work: No Facebook, tweeting, texting, phone calls, Internet surfing, fantasy football, etc. Do your personal things at lunch or after work—just do a great job.

4. *What should I be careful of when working with staffing agencies?*

It's important to be judicious in how you work with them. When working with staffing agencies and recruiters it's important that they not send your resume to a company for a role without your permission first. There are multiple reasons you want to have this understanding up front:

(a) You may not want to apply because it's a bad fit.

(b) You may have a better connection into that company. There are fantastic recruiters in the market who have rock-solid relationships with hiring managers and HR teams. This type of recruiter can be tremendously valuable to you in getting hired. There are also recruiters who do not have more than an acquaintance with a company you want to apply to. If this is a contingent recruiter it's entirely possible you have a closer connection inside the company. A target company of yours may open up a position you're ideal for and you may have a friend who works at the company, knows the hiring manager, and can present you to them as a candidate. If the contingent recruiter has only met or talked to the hiring manager once or twice they're going to have less influence with the hiring manager than your friend.

I'm often asked by people doing a search, why someone they know inside a company would want to advocate for them and present their resume. If it's a good friend of yours they'll want to do it to help a friend. But many companies offer a finder's fee of a couple thousand dollars to employees that bring in candidates that end up getting hired.

(c) The company may not have the budget to pay a contingency fee for a role that's an excellent fit for you. Many companies have tight budgets and this could prevent you getting hired at that company. Instead, the company may have to keep searching for a candidate where they won't have to pay a recruiter's fee even if the candidate isn't as excellent a fit as you.

Now let's say you've got an interview coming up and you're not sure how to prepare for it. If you feel it's potentially a bull's eye fit for you, you're going to use Step Seven to out-prepare your competition.

Summary

Chapter 14: A staffing agency is hired by companies to fill jobs for them because the company doesn't have the time, personnel, or expertise to do it for themselves. These temporary roles typically last anywhere from a day to months. And in some cases they can be full-time, which is how a staffing agency is different from a temp agency.

- To increase your likelihood of turning a short-term assignment into a full-time job, do the best possible job when at the company and build the strongest relationships you can.
- When working with staffing agencies and recruiters it's important that they not send your resume to a company for a role without your permission first.

Step Seven: Out-Prepare Your Competition

Nine out of ten job seekers don't know these critical preparation steps. Here's how to look like a rock star in your cover letter, resume, and interview.

Chapter 15: Take a Deep Breath Before You Jump: The Hidden Costs of Switching Companies

Francine loved her boss, Julia. Julia was inspirational, smart, strategic, fun, funny, and she challenged Francine to be better every single day in a supportive way. Julia got big things done at her company. Not small wins, but big wins that gave her a prominent position in the company. And Julia had style. She just always seemed to have it together, and when she didn't she just laughed at herself. That only raised Francine's esteem of Julia even further. But one day Julia quit and Francine took it hard. Really hard.

Francine hadn't met her new boss yet, but she had already decided she wouldn't like him as much as she liked Julia. How could she? So, with this chip on her shoulder she met her new boss and had to admit he was smart and strategic, but he was not fun or funny. What's more, Francine and her teammates were very quantitative and their new boss wasn't. Francine's language was numbers, but her new boss's language was customer perception and this frustrated Francine. When confronting a problem at work Francine wanted to know the numbers first; Francine's new boss wanted to know feelings first. Yes, feelings. "Lightweight," thought Francine.

In Francine's mind her new boss was on trial and the verdict could go either way, but it wasn't looking good for his defense. Finally, the tipping point was reached. Francine had a meeting with her new boss in which her boss told her that he was going to make a big strategic change. Francine thought the change was a bad idea. That was the last, damning piece of evidence for the prosecution. The defendant was guilty as charged. Francine contacted me that day to say she needed help. She had decided she was going to quit and wanted help navigating her exit. She wanted out. Fast.

We've all been there, right? We get fed up with our boss or we don't get the promotion or raise we expected so we say to ourselves and friends, "Screw it—I'm quitting this company and joining another." Step Seven is about out-preparing your competition to get hired in your next job. But if you're currently working, I want you to be certain that leaving your current company is your best career move. I don't want you to become one of those cautionary tales of regret: "Here toils poor Francine in accounting, she's in a sad slump; turns out her last firm wasn't so bad, but she had to jump." Is this really the right time for you to switch jobs? What if your current ecosystem is better than you realize? What if the absolutely best thing you can in this age of job-hopping is stay right where you are?

If you can't work out a good situation on your current team, please try to look inside your current company to see if there are opportunities on other teams or divisions that would be an excellent fit for you. I frequently coach people who change teams at their current company and it's as if the storm broke. All of sudden they're enjoying their company again and they don't have to ramp up a job search.

Many people end up switching jobs during their career—typically multiple times. There's debate about how often this actually happens today, but most current data have people working at four to seven companies during their career. The problem is that most people underestimate both the visible and the hidden costs of switching jobs.

HERE ARE THE MOST COMMON QUESTIONS I GET ABOUT LEAVING ONE COMPANY FOR ANOTHER

1. *What are the most common reasons people decide to change jobs and companies?*

- Number one reason that people quit their jobs: “People leave managers not companies” (Gallup) and according to Florida State Research “40% of employees work for bad bosses.” Sometimes we have to stay in a job for the paycheck. Sometimes we can change groups. Sometimes we can see that a bad boss is about to be transferred or fired. But if none of these apply, life’s too short to work for a bad boss.

- People don’t like their company culture. Maybe the culture doesn’t excite you or maybe it does, but there’s a deep character flaw in the culture. One man I coached was at a company who had a mission he felt passionate about. But this company also had culture that promoted backstabbers into executive positions. As a result, good people left the company and it was getting harder to hire excellent replacements as word got around.

- Lack of advancement opportunities. This became a problem during the Great Recession. There was a whole generation of senior managers and executives planning to retire, or at least move to part time, when they lost a big part of their retirement savings during the crash. Sadly, they had to put their retirement plans on hold for financial reasons and this created a lack of advancement opportunities for the people who were expecting to take over their boss’s job. Additionally, there are whole industries that have been going through challenging times, like much of the legal services industry, which has created few advancement opportunities for many lawyers.

- People feel unfulfilled. Sometimes people think they're going to love that new job and they realize it's not satisfying. Maybe they're in the right job, but at the wrong company.

- They want a career transition. Maybe they've worked in corporate finance their entire career, but they've always wanted to work in venture capital. Maybe they've worked in manufacturing their entire career, but now they're in the twilight of their career and before they retire they want to work for a non-profit and leave a legacy by advocating for wildlife preservation.

2. *You say that if I'm considering leaving a job that it's important to consider both the visible and the hidden costs of making that change. What costs are you talking about?*

According to the sexily named Bureau of Labor and Statistics, on average across all industries, employer-paid benefits make up about 30% of total compensation. 30%!

And yet when people jump to new companies they often don't take these into account. It's common where an employee will get a new job with a higher salary, but benefits are so much lower that their total compensation can actually be lower.

When I say benefits I mean a variety of things like stock options, health care, insurance, bonuses, vacation, commuting reimbursement, etc.

The following is not meant to be an exhaustive list, but here are some of the visible costs someone contemplating moving to a new company should think through:

- Vesting of stock options. I was coaching a marketing manager at a healthcare startup who had been at his company for eleven months and was thinking of leaving. He wanted to start a dialogue with his boss and I suggested that he not start that conversation until he "vested" his first year. Vesting means you've worked at the company for the required time necessary to be entitled to ownership of the options vested. If his boss didn't take kindly to the idea of him leaving, he might have let him go before he hit his one-year mark and he would have gotten zero of his options. So, make sure you know what your situation is and consider lost value in your decision.

- 401 (k). Check with your target company to find out if you can start contributing to your plan immediately or if you have to wait. Also, some companies require you to be vested before they start matching, so clarify that, too. And find out if you can take all, or just part, of your 401(k) if you leave your current company. Determine if your new company does 401 (k) matching. If your current company does and your new company doesn't that can cost you thousands of tax-free dollars every year that are currently being given to you.

- Retirement pensions. One client I was coaching worked for a well-known pharma company and she got a small pension upon her five year anniversary, but a much more significant pension upon her ten year anniversary, which she made. If she'd left after nine and a half years she would have lost that significant jump. But now she has peace of mind in knowing that upon retirement she will have a significant pension income, which is increasingly rare these days.

- Annual bonuses. Many companies that give annual bonuses only give them if you've been working there for the past year and you're still currently working there. If your current company gives out an annual bonus in January and you leave in December you may not get anything.

- Healthcare coverage. This is one of the most important benefits on which to do the math, since the amount you'll have to contribute can vary significantly between companies. Your coverage will vary, too. Some companies offer vision care while others don't. One man I was coaching received an offer from a company he very much wanted to work for, but he was disappointed that the base salary was lower than he expected. He felt it was lower than market rate, so he was thinking of not taking the offer. We talked through the healthcare benefits they offered and he realized they were amazingly generous—easily among the top 10% of healthcare benefits offered by other companies. After he did the math he realized that just focusing on base salary was a misleading number. The more critical number was his total compensation. With healthcare factored in, this offer was in fact market rate. He took the job the next morning and loves it there.

- Healthcare reimbursement. Most companies have different healthcare reimbursement amounts, so know what those levels are in both your current and your target company.

- Childcare. When I did an internship at SC Johnson during graduate school they had recently opened up on-site childcare. It was high quality and subsidized, so working parents were thrilled to have this benefit. Not only where employees' children in a caring environment, but employees could also pop over to check on their children during the day.

- Tuition/degree reimbursement. Much like healthcare reimbursement, most companies have varying levels of tuition reimbursement, so find out what your current and target company offers. The much bigger ticket item is degree reimbursement. There were a number of classmates of mine at Kellogg who were having their MBA paid for by their company. The agreement was that upon graduation the employee would go back to work for the company, typically from three to five years. Contracts vary, but for most employees if they leave early and do not stay for the agreed length of time, the employee has to pay a pro-rated amount of tuition back to the company. As an example, tuition alone at Kellogg is over $56,000 per year. If an employee graduated from the two year MBA program and then chose to go work for another company, they'd owe the company over $112,000.

- Food reimbursement. When I worked at CREDO Mobile we had a subsidized cafeteria because our offices were in a Federal building. Ok, the food wasn't gourmet, but it was fine and saved me at least $3–$4 every day. Over the course of the year that translated into savings of at least $600.

- Vacation. Companies vary in their vacation offerings. The important thing to focus on is your total vacation time and what you may or may not lose. Many companies give you vacation pay based on how long you've been at the company. If you've been at your present company for ten years and then join a startup, you may be going from four weeks of paid vacation to two weeks unless you negotiate otherwise.

- Cell phone reimbursement. Yahoo! made news last year when they announced that they were giving a free smartphone to their full-time employees. They're also paying for employees' phone bills (voice and data usage). So, not only do employees get a free iPhone 5 or Android phone, but they also get their monthly bills paid for. For a smartphone with a monthly bill of $100 that's an additional annual benefit for every employee of $1,200.

- Taxes. People often don't remember that their city or county taxes can change based on where they work. If you take a new job and move to a new city are you increasing your taxes significantly?
- Commuting costs. Some people go from walking to work or taking the bus to having to drive over an hour. Now they have to pay for gas and maintenance. Perhaps an even bigger commuting cost is the emotional toll an increased commute can take on us. One woman I coached loves her job, loves her boss, loves her company, loves her compensation and hates her commute. Round trip it takes her over two hours every day and three on Fridays. That's time she doesn't get to spend with her husband and daughter.
- Dress. I live in San Francisco, the birthplace of casual dress in the workplace. Casual dress has a lot of benefits—we're more comfortable and don't have to buy expensive suits or dresses because they're required by the company code. And that's before dry cleaning! I've worked at companies where it was common to see colleagues walking around in shorts or barefoot. At one company we had a well-dressed French colleague visiting and upon seeing a barefooted employee walk by he burst out with "It's true! You really go barefoot here—I thought it was just in the movies!" I couldn't tell if his reaction was positive amazement or contemptuous disdain. One woman I coached is an excellent dresser. Then she joined a new company in the Bay Area and to her surprise found herself surrounded by colleagues in HQ wearing designer labels. New York City, sure. But the Bay Area? In the end, though, company culture trumps city culture. This very professionally dressed woman felt compelled to further upgrade her wardrobe, which cost her over $2,000.

- Sabbatical. Sounds like a fantasy, right? But according to a SHRM (Society for Human Resource Management) poll, 5% of American companies offer paid sabbaticals and 18% offer unpaid sabbaticals. McDonald's offers sabbaticals and a friend of mine who works at Charles Schwab took an amazing sabbatical and came back re-energized and feeling more creative than ever. It also increased her loyalty to Schwab.

That's a long list, right? But these are just the visible costs!

People often don't think about the hidden or invisible costs of joining a new company such as the extra time and effort it'll take you to:

- Learn a new corporate culture, which can easily take a year. Sure, the grass is always greener, but after you get into that new company your previous company might not look so dysfunctional by comparison. As one woman contemplating a jump said, "At least at my current company I know where the bodies are buried."

- Learn how the new systems and processes work in the new company. Does your new company use a different kind of online meeting tool? A new email system?

- Learn a new boss. Yes, your current boss make be ticking you off because she sometimes steals credit for your work, but your next boss might be a belittler and make your current boss look a lot better by comparison.

- Learn your new teammates. Joe sure seemed like a nice guy when he interviewed you, but now you're learning that he's very territorial. How are you going to navigate that?

- Build new relationships with people throughout the company. In your last company you had your short-list of people you knew you could trust—people who would give you a heads up to protect you from some corporate storm on the horizon. You'll have to build new relationships to create that same early-warning system at your new company.

- Build new relationships with new corporate partners and vendors. Let's say you're a sales rep. At your last company you knew you could always pick up the phone and call a few trusted partners to get enough end-of-quarter sales to hit your quota. Now you're working in a related, but separate industry and you don't have those same relationships yet.

- Learning how to find work/life balance in your new company. You've always worked hard, maybe too hard. But in your current company your boss travels a lot and when she's not in the office on Fridays you work from home to catch up on email and to re-charge. But your new boss may dislike people working from home, so you'll lose that opportunity to re-energize. How are you going to avoid burnout?

- You've built up your personal brand in your current company and you'll have to rebuild that from scratch in your next company. Your current boss's boss knows you sometimes finish projects late, but your finished product is always excellent. Now in your new job, all your boss's boss sees is that you're late. You don't have a personal brand built with her, so she doesn't know you're going to deliver great work and this might cause you problems.

Many people who want to jump ship often discover that the best thing they can do is to stay right where they are. So, before you decide to leave your current situation make a list of all the reasons you should:

- Move on to another job.
- Stay right where you are.

It's important to keep in mind that an effective way to transition into a new job is to excel so completely that your company finds you indispensable and a high performer they want to promote.

3. *Can you give us a few tips on things we can do to make life better at our current jobs, so we are happier without having to make a change?*

Of course it totally depends on what your source of frustration is at work, but some of the most common problems include:

- Your boss. If you can't work it out, try to move to a new group within your company.
- Working crazy hours or dealing with a grueling commute. One man I was coaching was on the verge of quitting solely due to his commute. His boss was sympathetic, so he was able to work from home one day a week. He wanted two, but it was a start and it made an unbearable commute bearable.
- Feeling your job security threatened by a new junior report. Instead of viewing this up-and-comer as a threat, view them as an opportunity. You now have enough staffing to launch that new program you're certain will work, add a lot of value to your company, and be a big win for you. It might even lead to that promotion you're on track for. And do you remember all those annoying parts of your job you've dreamed of

unloading? Unload them to your junior report! Create your ideal job description where you take the most important and interesting requirements, have your junior report do the rest, and you two can work together to be the most successful team possible. These newer heights and possibly even your promotion wouldn't be possible for you without your junior report.

After experiencing all of these switching costs, people often regret leaving their current company and look back longingly while thinking "it was an insane asylum, but it was my insane asylum."

Of course there are times when it's better to leave your current company. But before making that jump, if you're on the edge of quitting your current company because your boss didn't give you recognition for your latest win, take a deep breath and make a serious effort to work things out. You might be glad you did. You may be in a better ecosystem than you realize. And if you're not, if you ultimately decide you need a new ecosystem to thrive, isn't it worth the effort to gain that certainty?

You don't want to just jump and take the first job that comes along without doing your preparation to figure out what you truly want to do next strategically. Otherwise you may find yourself in the same situation in a year. But if you have that certainty that it's time for you to leave, then it's time to kick ass with your preparation to get hired. That's what I cover in the next chapter on how to out-prepare.

Summary

Step Seven. Chapter 15: If you're currently working at a company and are thinking of leaving, be certain that leaving is your best next career move. Ask yourself these questions: Is this really the right time to switch jobs? What if my current ecosystem is better than I realize?

- If you can't work out a good situation on your current team, try to look internally to see if there are any opportunities on other teams at your company that would be an excellent fit for you.
- The #1 reason people quit their jobs is their boss. According to research done by Gallup, "People leave managers not companies" and Florida State University research founds that "40% of employees work for bad bosses".
- There are multiple visible and hidden costs most people underestimate when leaving one company to join another.
- Many people who are thinking of leaving their company often discover that the best thing they can do is to stay right where they are.

Chapter 16: How to Turn Your Preparation into a Competitive Advantage: Cover Letters, Resumes, and Interviewing

I've worked so hard for this and to be able to get the gold medal is so awesome. I've given up everything for this. It means everything to me. It's why I work hard; it's why I'm in the gym every day.

Lindsey Vonn, the world's greatest female skier, after winning a gold medal at the Olympics

WORLD-CLASS PREPARATION

You find a job opportunity that is really interesting and it's important to you to get the interview. In addition to finding any connections you have to the hiring manager, you're going to need an outstanding cover letter and resume, and you need to wow the company during your interview. Most job search books talk about the mechanics of cover letters, resumes, and interviewing. While mechanics are important, I want to focus on a new path, one that's not often covered, at least not in the depth to which I'm going to cover it.

That path is focusing on the two most important things you control between this moment and the interview: Your mindset and your preparation. I guided you through mindset in Step One and now it's time to learn how to out-prepare. I'm not talking about normal, cursory preparation. I'm talking about Lindsey Vonn-like preparation —the kind of world-class preparation that'll elevate your cover letter, resume and interviewing and leave your competition in the dust. I'm talking about you being the best-prepared candidate your hiring manager meets.

Remember to control your controllables. You don't control if the hiring manager interviewing you doesn't like the angle you're sitting at in your chair. You don't control whom you're competing against for the job. But you control your preparation. It took me years to figure this out, but after I did I learned that by out-preparing myself for my interview I actually did control my job search. In the last couple of job searches I did I never had to interview with more than three or four companies before getting a job I was very excited about.

After hearing how much preparation I recommend for job interviews, people frequently say "but if I don't get that job isn't all my preparation a waste of time?" I don't view it as a waste—I view it as an investment.

Even though I highly recommend intense preparation as a critical job search method, I do put one important boundary around it. I only out-prepare for jobs at companies I consider a great fit, and that usually means three or four per job search. If I have an interview for a job I'm interested in but don't think it's an excellent fit, I do not do intense preparation—I'll just do a couple of hours.

Let's focus on a job opportunity you're excited about. Here's how you out-prepare to elevate your cover letter, resume and interviewing, and leave your competition in the dust.

THREE LEVELS OF COVER LETTERS

In this day of Linkedin and recruiters, many people wonder if cover letters even matter anymore. They absolutely do. By following my advice below you'll be able to write a cover letter and resume that stands out.

Let's start with cover letters. Everything below is direct feedback from hiring managers who have explained what gets them to ask an applicant for their resume and a phone or in-person interview.

Level 1: The Form Email

This is a form cover letter sent by applicants that is so generic it appears as if the candidate is using the same cover letter to apply for countless other jobs, which is obvious because sometimes they forget to update the name of the company they're applying to. It's not personalized in any way and is normally sent to the digital wastebasket by the hiring manager.

Level 2: The Keyword Reverse Engineer

This applicant has at least read the job posting and identified the keywords important to the company. That's obvious because if the job posting said that "leadership experience" and "project management" are two critical skills the company is looking for, then the applicant "reverse engineers" their cover letter and talks about these specific keywords. Of course this is a better cover letter than the form email, but all the candidate is doing is plugging in keywords. This cover letter is boring, impersonal and it's clear the applicant doesn't understand the organization's culture.

Level 3: The Rock Star

This person has clearly researched the organization. They get the culture and use specific examples to prove that. They have high emotional intelligence, and they're not just pulling keywords from the job description. They authentically communicate their passion for the job they're applying for and tie it into their story in a way that makes complete sense that this job is exactly what they should be doing next. They also give clear examples of how they've added value in previous jobs and are able to relate how those previous successes will translate into success in your company. At most 10% of applicants are at this level. These are the candidates that stand out and who are most likely to be asked in for an interview. Hiring managers are impressed to receive their cover letters and excited to meet these rock stars. This is you.

RESUME WRITING FOR RESPONSE

If you write a rock star cover letter you'll impress the hiring manager and they will read your resume. Now you need to make sure you've written a great resume. Since there are so many excellent resume-writing books out there, I'm not going to drill down into those mechanics. Instead, I want to focus on the most important strategic factors.

My coaches and I review good resumes all the time that an excellent resume service or talented university career center coach helped the client write. If the client used a resume writing service they may be paying $400–$2,000 plus. If the client is a student they're getting that valuable coaching for free from their career center. But, unfortunately, only a small percentage of the resumes we review are excellent. To write an outstanding resume, please have this mindset:

- Your resume is a critical asset in your personal branding. Your brand is made up of a variety of factors with you, your record of success, and your reputation at the center of it all.

When applying to a company, three of your assets include your cover letter, Linkedin profile, and resume. An essential component of personal branding is consistency, so you want all three of your assets to tell the same story. I've evaluated candidates who wrote a great cover letter and a great Linkedin profile, but didn't update their resume to match them. It's jarring when this happens and it decreases the likelihood of that candidate moving forward.

- Just like there are three levels of cover letters, the same is true for resumes. I've advertised many job openings during my career and most applicants submitted resumes that felt like spam. I'd ask for five critical skills and people would apply even if they didn't have any of those skills. Then there's the keyword reverse engineer who uses the keywords I used in the online job posting, but their experience doesn't back up the keywords. You want to write a rock star resume to match your rock star cover letter. To achieve this, your resume has to be customized for the job you're applying for, as I explain below. You don't have the time do this for every job you apply for, but you need to tailor it for a job you're passionate about and one for which you feel you're a bull's eye fit.

- Tell your story in a compelling way that fits the job you're applying for. The fundamental problem with most resumes is that they don't tell a story. Moreover, after reading them, hiring managers often don't see why the candidate is an excellent fit for this exact job at their company.

- Communicate your cultural and skill-set fit. Since HR leaders are looking for both in candidates, be sure to highlight these points in your resume. For example, if through your research of the company you've gotten to know their culture as highly collaborative, then mention in your resume "team oriented professional."

- Start with your summary statement immediately underneath your name and contact information. This is a point of debate inside the resume-writing world. Some people say it's a waste of space to include a summary statement because all it is doing is repeating what's below it in the resume. I fiercely disagree. Summary statements are critical because they give you the opportunity to tell your story in a few sentences. Many HR leaders, recruiters, and hiring managers I work with read the summary statement first and if it doesn't feel like a super fit they won't read the resume at all.

- Own your expertise. If you're early in your career you at least have experience in a certain area and you may already have expertise. If you're mid or late-career you have expertise in a least one and possibly multiple areas. And yet you'd be surprised by how many people don't own their experience or expertise. For all the fun people have poking fun about how Americans view themselves as gurus and are happy to proclaim that from the mountain tops, the fact is most Americans are modest and don't feel comfortable fully owning their expertise for fear of coming off as arrogant. Of course you don't want to overstate your expertise or come off as too strong, but you have to own and communicate your expertise in all of your assets and most importantly during your interviews. If you don't, you'll give a false impression to the hiring manager. You'll communicate a fraction of the real you and your chances of getting hired will be a fraction of what they should be.

- Communicate what you personally achieved, not what your company achieved. Yes, it's helpful to give a sense of perspective and scale for the organizations you've worked at, such as "product manager at a $7 billion healthcare leader." But in your resume your focus should be on what you achieved. For example, if you personally led the introduction of a new product last year, instead of saying "part of a medical devices company that grew 35% last year," highlight your personal accomplishment by saying, "launched a new medical device that drove 15% of corporate growth."

- Quantify your impressive results whenever possible. Your resume is a story, but a story is more impactful if it includes some "wow" quantified results. As a customer service manager you may have "improved customer service," but it's more impressive to quantify your achievement and say, "increased customer satisfaction by 28%." I often hear from some professionals that they are in positions where their progress can't be quantified. This normally isn't the case, though, because there are numerous ways to quantify and communicate superlatives. For example, I've had product managers say they cannot quantify their work but then realize they can say things like "launched a new product that increased revenue 12%," or "decreased launch time by two months."

- Know every detail of your resume. You've been interviewing for a few weeks and every conversation has focused on your most recent positions. Then in your next interview the hiring manager notices your first job from fifteen years ago because he worked at the same company, so he asks you about that job. The problem is you forgot that job was even on your resume! You have "wow" answers regarding every recent position, but you stumble through this question because you never talk about your oldest one. This happens frequently. If you have something on your resume, anything, be prepared to talk about it.

- Keep it up to date. Crafting a great resume is hard work that takes multiple iterations. That's why it is so important to keep it up to date. If you suddenly start a job search it can weeks before you have an excellent resume. But if you are always keeping it up to date by adding in your latest accomplishments, you'll be able to have it in fighting form in days, not weeks.

- Incredibly important for college graduates. Of course resumes are important for all professionals, but this is especially true for recent college graduates. This is natural because they don't have much work experience. That's why for college graduates who have done an internship, it's important to include that valuable work experience on your resume and to clearly highlight your achievements from that internship.

- Regarding length, if you're a recent college graduate it shouldn't be more than one page. For all other managers and executives it's best to not be more than two pages unless you're in the C-suite. I've seen plenty of CEOs, CTOs and CMOs with resumes that are two pages or two and a half pages and that's all they need. But a manager or director should not have a resume that's three pages or longer. Recruiters simply don't have the time to wade through a resume that long, nor do they need that much detail.

- Customize your resume into three or four versions depending on what you're applying for. You choose what to highlight in your resume and what experiences to include. For example, if you are a management consultant who has worked in a variety of industries, you want to customize your resume for the main industries you're applying to. If you're applying for a healthcare job then you want to have a version of your resume that highlights your healthcare experience from your consulting. Ditto for financial services etc.

INTERVIEWING TO WIN

Your cover letter and resume impressed so much the company asked you to come in for an interview. Here are the benefits you'll get by preparing so much for your interview. You will:

- Be more likely to get the job offer you truly want and find more fulfilling.
- Shorten the total length of your job search.
- Find out faster if you truly love the company or not. I've done intense preparation before for an interview and realized I didn't want to work at the company, so I took myself out of the running. Yes, I spent two days preparing for a one-hour interview, but if I hadn't, I might have taken the job and only found out after I was at the company that it wasn't a cultural fit for me.
- Impress the people with whom you interview much more, which oftentimes leads to higher salaries. A hiring manager will not go to bat with HR for higher compensation if they feel the person they're giving the offer to is a good fit, but not great. But if you wow the hiring manager and you become their #1 choice they'll frequently fight internally to get you on

board. I know because I've fought for people when I was hiring.

- Increase the likelihood of getting introductions to other companies if you don't get the job at this company because they'll be so impressed by your preparation.
- Impress the recruiter who got you the interview. So, even if you don't get that job they'll keep you at the top of their list when other opportunities come up. Remember, you reflect on the recruiter when you go to the company for your interview. You affect not only your brand, but theirs, too. Even if the company decides to hire someone else there's a good chance the hiring manager will let the recruiter know how impressed they were by your preparation and insights. That'll give the recruiter the confidence to send you, rather than your competition, out to other interviews.

How to Out-Prepare Yourself over Your Competitors and Win the Job

Your preparation will vary based on the type of job you're interviewing for, the company culture, and the industry. But here's the preparation framework I coach people on using.

Step 1: Know the ecosystem you thrive best in.

Meaning, do as much self-reflection and research as you can to know yourself, your future boss, your target company, and your best timing.

Step 2: Research your target company:

- Do they have an impressive executive team?
- Are they a leader or a Top 3 player in their space? If not, do they have a specific plan to leapfrog their competitors? If not, they may not have long-lasting financial strength and may not be around for long.
- Are they financially strong? If they're a startup, are they well funded?

Step 3: Do a deeper dive to out-prepare your competition.

This is what will separate you from your competition. Your goal here is to be the best-prepared candidate they interview.

- If you're interviewing at a public company, read their annual report on their website. By doing so you'll gain a fast understanding of the company, its strengths and weaknesses. Read their report to find strategic insights relevant to the job you're interviewing for and bring your points up during your interview. A friend of mine used to work at a leading management consulting firm. The firm had built as part of their culture the practice that all consultants had to read the annual report of a potential client before meeting them.
- Tell the people interviewing you something they don't know about their company, product, competitors, or industry. By

adding value during your interview you'll prove that you'll add value once you're working at the company.

- Do deep preparation regarding the job you're interviewing for so you can give strategic insights during your interviews. For example, let's say you're interviewing for a finance job at a public company. Do a financial analysis of the company's annual report and financial statements. They should be available on their corporate website. You'll get strategic insights from your research and during your interview bring them up like this: "I analyzed your financial statements as part of my preparation for meeting with you and I noticed that Cost of Goods Sold (COGS) % went up last year and that it's now higher than your two biggest competitors. Was this strategically planned or was it unplanned? If it was unexpected, is there a plan in place now to reduce COGS?"

- If the company sells products or services be sure to test them if at all possible. They may have product functionality on their website you can review. If they have an app be sure to download the app and use the product on your phone or tablet. Sometimes software can be expensive, so if you're interviewing at a software company see if they have a free trial you can sign up for and evaluate.

- When I interviewed for one executive position the hiring manager asked me for a couple of slides to summarize my strategic insights. I put together a six-page presentation that included the following:

    - Marketing overview of the most important success drivers to achieve the company's growth goal.

- Online marketing review that compared the company against their two biggest competitors' products. My chart evaluated the strengths and weaknesses of each company's Facebook, Twitter, YouTube, blogging, search engine optimization (SEO), search engine marketing (SEM), affiliate marketing and email marketing campaigns. My summary highlighted the opportunities for the company.
- User experience review that compared the company against their two biggest competitors. Like my online marketing channel review, I listed a summary that highlighted the opportunities for the company regarding how they could improve their user experience.

In total it took me three days to complete my strategic analysis and it was worth every minute. My preparation was a critical factor in getting hired. I do not recommend doing such an in-depth analysis for every company you interview at—who has the time?! But if you believe you've found an ecosystem you will thrive in and a job you feel is a superb fit, then you have to be #1 in preparation. Even when you do go the extra mile in preparation you will not get an offer from every company you do this sort of preparation for. It has normally worked for me, but it has not worked every single time. There were two companies where I did this level of preparation and I came in a close second. In both cases I later saw the Linkedin profile of the person they hired and in both cases the woman they hired had more relevant experience for the job. So, while I was disappointed not to get an offer, if I was the hiring manager I would have made the same choice. But those have been the exceptions. The norm has been that I've gotten the offer through my preparation. My preparation has given me another benefit, too. Years ago I found doing a job search to be an endless source of stress and anxiety.

But once I started preparing at this higher level my stress dropped immediately. That's because it fundamentally changes the dynamics of your meeting. It no longer feels like an "interview" where you have lower status because you're hoping you'll do a good job of answering the traditional interview questions ("Tell me your three biggest strengths and weaknesses"). Instead, your preparation will transform the interview into a conversation of equals. You'll walk into your meeting confident, knowing you're going to give the hiring manager valuable insights into their own business that they didn't have before. And that's a beautiful thing.

Clients ask me all the time, "When will I know I'm done preparing?" I can tell when they're done because most clients go through three phases in their preparation:

- Searching for their story and key points they want to make during their interview. People in this first phase are in their research period. They're gathering potential stories and success highlights they might want to communicate.

- Half-owning their story in their own words. This second phase is where you start to see the framework for their compelling story emerging, but they're often still thinking through most questions, so it doesn't quite feel natural yet.

- Mastery of their story and a clear plan to communicate their key points that came out of their preparation. It's not until this last step that I usually see the fully confident client. I also know they've reached mastery of their story when they naturally tell it instead of tripping over parts of it, which fogs their underlying expertise. This point is also when their expertise fully shines through because they've found their voice. It's almost like meeting a different person because in their mastery phase they're confident, focused, and able to naturally communicate their deep experience—and that's exciting to witness. This is when I know I'm not needed anymore and that's a great feeling for me.

Ask Strategic Questions at the End of Your Interview

I need to make one final point about interviewing, which is the importance of asking great questions at the end of your interview. Certainly, ask them during your interview, but always be prepared to ask at least four or five more at the end, assuming the interviewer isn't cutting off that opportunity due to time constraints. Hiring managers have told me they've eliminated candidates from consideration solely because they didn't ask any questions at the end of the interview. The types of questions you want to ask vary by job type, company, and industry. But broadly speaking, here are suggestions you can choose from to get you started:

- How would you describe your company culture?
- What are the company's most important goals over the next year?
- How would you describe your leadership style?
- For the person that ends up in this role, what would they have to achieve in the next six to twelve months for you to believe they're adding a lot of value?
- Is there anything in my experience that you feel I'm missing to be very successful in this role? Some people love asking this question. If the hiring manager has a concern, it gives the candidate the opportunity to learn that before they leave so they can answer that doubt. But some candidates don't feel

comfortable being this direct. Do what you're comfortable with.

I know you are probably surprised at the amount of preparation I've done to get jobs. You may never have gone to that extent for a job you'd love to have. I hope that you know deep down out-preparing is the right thing to do. If you'd love to have the job then why wouldn't you do anything to get it? I know many of you will out-prepare and significantly increase your chances of getting hired. Please email me your success stories.

Now let's assume you got the offer. That's awesome, but you still need to negotiate your offer. Next I'm going to walk you through the final step, which is Step Eight: Close Your Offer.

Summary

Chapter 16: When you have an interview for an opportunity you're excited about your goal is to be the best-prepared candidate the hiring manager meets.

- Of course there are multiple factors you do not control during a job search. But you control 100% of your preparation for an interview.
- Cover letters are still important. There are three levels of cover letters: The form email, the keyword reverse engineer, and the rock star. Be the rock star that you are.
- Even with the rise in importance of Linkedin profiles, resumes are still critical. Your resume is an important digital asset not only in your job search, but also as part of your personal branding.

- By out-preparing you'll be more likely to get the job offer you truly want and find more fulfilling. You'll also be more likely to shorten the total length of your job search.
- If you're interviewing at a public company always be sure to read their annual report beforehand.
- Be sure to ask strategic questions at the end of your interview. Your questions should focus on learning more about the company culture, company and team goals, as well as details about the role and responsibilities of the job you're interviewing for.

Step Eight: Close Your Offer

How to successfully negotiate a package you're happy with (and maybe even live happily ever after!).

Chapter 17: How to Negotiate Your Job Offer from a Position of Strength

You did it. You grew your connections, your preparation for your interviews was off the charts, you wowed your interviewers and now you're getting the job offer you wanted.

This should be the most exciting part of the whole job search process, right? Not necessarily, because negotiating drives most people's anxiety levels through the roof. Why? A person about to get an offer feels that the end of the often-painful job search is finally over. You can see the finish line and you don't want to blow it, which is understandable. The other anxiety-causing part of negotiation is that most people would rather clean their oven than negotiate their own offer. Don't get me wrong—these same people when negotiating for their company will display shark-like tenacity squeezing every last dollar out of a deal. But for themselves? Not so much. Most people find it far easier to negotiate for other people or a company than for themselves.

HERE ARE THE MOST COMMON NEGOTIATION QUESTIONS I GET FROM CLIENTS

1. *How do I successfully negotiate a package I'm happy with?*

   The critical factor in negotiating a higher offer is to focus on market rate, your skills, your experience, and how much value you will bring to the company.

2. *Why negotiate?*

The answer to the question "why negotiate?" probably sounds obvious, right? We want more money! But it's more complex than that. I've had friends before who were financially stressed and didn't want to risk losing the offer, so they accepted it on the spot and that was the right answer for them. But if you're not in that situation or some other extenuating circumstance, then you should always negotiate. There are numerous reasons to do so:

You'll make a higher base salary.

If your company offers bonuses they will be higher because bonuses are typically based off of your base salary.

It sets a higher base for your future raises.

It sets a higher base for future companies you work for.

It's good practice for future negotiations.

It builds respect from your manager.

It's an indication of your worth to the company.

One time before founding I was negotiating my fee for a consulting project with a large company and I had a great call with the hiring manager. She asked me for my hourly rate and I hadn't done my homework regarding what was the latest market rate, so I gave her a lowball rate to be safe. The moment she heard my rate I could feel the air go out of our conversation. She assumed that because my rate was lower than expected my expertise was lower, too. I didn't get the project because I asked for too little.

3. *Who should I negotiate with?*

You're prepared to negotiate, but before you do remember to do this first: Thank the person who is giving you the offer and express your excitement about joining the company. After you've done that, the big question is, "Who should I negotiate with?" Normally offers are negotiated with the hiring manager or HR department, but I've also negotiated offers with co-founders I didn't report to. At another company I even negotiated the basic parameters of my compensation with an executive recruiter and then the final details with the hiring manager.

In most cases you want to negotiate with the hiring manager because they can be your biggest advocate. If you need to push, though, remember that you'll have an ongoing relationship with the hiring manager. You need to read the hiring manager's reactions to make sure you're not pushing too far. One executive told me that after joining a company and becoming a rock star there, he got feedback that they almost pulled his offer because he negotiated so aggressively.

If you do need to push, it's best to push the HR manager because in most cases you won't have an ongoing relationship with them. The other important person you may have to deal with is the recruiter, who will typically ask you your compensation expectations up front to make sure you're in the compensation range of what the company wants to pay. Keep in mind that the recruiter works for the company, not you. Of course the higher your salary the higher the commission the recruiter makes. But, ultimately, the recruiter's loyalties lie with the company, because the company is paying them and recruiters want to build long-term relationships with companies.

So, in most cases you'll want to negotiate with your hiring manager.

4. *When should I negotiate?*

When you have the most power! You normally have the most power when you get the offer and know you're their first choice, which is a great feeling. So, try to delay the compensation discussion until the end. If it's early in the interviewing process and the hiring or HR manager asks you what your expectations are, try a response like this: "I'm more focused on job fit. I'm sure this job will have a competitive package and I'd prefer to talk about that when we know each other better."

Some companies will persist, and if you can't dodge the question anymore give a range of what your expectations are instead of stating exactly what your base salary was at your last company. Give a range of expectations that's higher than what you're currently making.

I should mention that with recruiters it's typically a different situation. They need to know you're at least in the ballpark of what their client can pay, so expect that question. Most of the executive recruiters I've dealt with accepted my range of base salary expectations and I can only think of one who let me dodge the question entirely before passing me to the company for the next round of interviewing.

I've hired hundreds of employees over the years and so long as an applicant is within the range of what my company can pay I don't care if one applicant is asking more than another. All I care about is finding the best employee who can add the most value to my company. In my career I've only had one interview not move forward because of compensation. I was a marketing director at the time and I was interviewing with an

Internet startup. It turned out they were not well funded and my base salary expectations were over $40,000 higher than their ability to pay. I was asking for a base salary that was market rate. We could have bridged a gap of $5,000–$10,000, but not $40,000, so we ended the interview in a friendly way.

Lastly, I've coached people over the years who almost took themselves out of the running early on because they found out the base salary was on the low end of what they expected. If you think the company, position, team and culture could be a good opportunity for you, please continue the dialogue. I've seen it time and time again where the company fell in love with a candidate through the interviewing process and raised the base salary significantly to get that candidate. But that can only happen if you negotiate when you have the most power, which is at the end of the process.

You got the offer and you accepted it. Congratulations! You worked hard to get hired. But you may also be in the enviable situation where you have to choose from more than one opportunity. If that's you, then read on to the next chapter to learn how to evaluate multiple opportunities.

Thanks to Matthew Temple, Director of Alumni Career Services for the Kellogg School of Management, for part of this content on negotiation. Thanks also to the Kellogg School of Management at Northwestern University.

Summary

Step 8. Chapter 17: The critical factor in negotiating a higher offer is to focus on market rate, your skills, your experience, and how much value you'll bring to the company.

- Some people have significant financial pressures and don't want to negotiate at all out of concern they may lose the offer. But for everyone else, there are multiple reasons to negotiate.
- Before you start negotiating first thank the person who gave you the offer and express your excitement about joining the company.
- In most cases you want to negotiate with the hiring manager because they can be your biggest advocate and likely control their own budget.
- You normally have the most negotiating power when you get the offer and know you're their first choice, which is a great feeling. So, try to delay the compensation discussion until the end.

Chapter 18: How to Evaluate Multiple Opportunities

After coaching numerous people during their process from starting a job search to getting hired, I can tell you there's a very common experience people go through. In the beginning of a search, when people are most vulnerable because they're not sure what direction to go in, job seekers live on a diet of stress for breakfast, anxiety for lunch, and worry for dinner. This is especially true for someone who was just fired, laid off, or who quit due to realizing the rocket ship of a company they thought they were joining turned out to be a clown car. Our inner critic feasts upon these negative experiences and it takes serious self-exploration to regain our equilibrium. I know what this feels like because, although I've had multiple successes over the years that I'm very proud of, I've also failed. I've made mistakes in my career that I've regretted. I've coached many people through this transformative period and it's not an easy place to be in initially, but it is often a portal to tremendous personal growth.

During the initial phase of a job search, it can often seem like the process will drag on forever, but then it will all come together with your right ecosystem and you'll get an offer you're excited about. You may end up with multiple opportunities because when it rains it pours job offers. One month you're having trouble sleeping at night because your inner critic is whispering in your ear that your job search will take longer than King Arthur's epic search for the sword in the stone; the next month you have two amazing job offers and you want to cut down your inner critic for putting you through that needless anxiety. Ironically, having multiple opportunities can be stressful, too. Certainly not as anxiety inducing as a layoff or a long job search, but it raises our stress levels nonetheless and we now stay awake at night asking ourselves, “What if I choose the wrong job?”

To choose between two opportunities, start by reviewing Step Two to evaluate which job offer will best enable you to optimize your personal ecosystem. Knowing yourself better than ever before, which future boss and company is a more optimal ecosystem for your excellence to thrive?

Additionally, rank the Top 5 decision factors from the list below that are most important to you:

- Job role and responsibilities. Does one offer more closely align to the ideal job role you want? Are you tired of making widgets and are you looking to make a difference?
- Stepping stone experience. When you think about the job you'd like to have after this next one, does one of your two offers better set you up for your career path?
- Influence over key decisions. If you are in a hierarchical culture you'll have less influence over key decisions. If you're in a flatter organization you'll normally have more. How important is this to you?
- Specific Industry. Is there a specific industry you are passionate about? Are both offers in that industry?
- Specific company. For years have you wanted to work at Apple, Proctor and Gamble or IDEO? Is there a cutting edge advertising agency you're passionate about joining like award-winning Rodgers Townsend in St. Louis that isn't a household name but is known by industry leaders and clients for its extraordinarily creative and impactful work? Maybe you dream of joining a non-profit that's making the world a better place, like Kiva ora smaller non-profit in your area.

- Company size. Do you thrive more in a roll-up-your sleeves small company with 40 employees or a large multinational company with 40 thousand employees where you'll have greater resources?

- Company culture. Please remember from Step Two, if you're evaluating offers from two different companies you're evaluating very different cultures.

- Relationship with your boss. Please also remember from Step Two that it's important to learn what type of managerial style your potential bosses have. Is one a delegator and the other a micro-manager?

- Total compensation. Compare the total compensation from your job offers. One offer might have a higher base salary, but lower total compensation when you add in bonus, stock options, and healthcare.

- Growth opportunities. If you have two job offers, is one of the companies growing faster than the other? If so, it'll give you greater opportunities over time. There are fast growing companies in every region of America and one of them may be your next employer.

- Travel. Some people want to travel and some quit their current jobs so they don't have to travel anymore. If you're willing to travel does one job require more of it? Intense travel can be particularly challenging for working parents.

- Creative freedom. Are you particularly creative? If so, do you need to have creative freedom in your job? I've coached creatives who took one job over another based on how much freedom they thought their future company would give them.

- Recognition. I've seen employees leave companies mainly because their boss or company never recognized their valuable contributions. Some companies offer greater opportunity for external recognition, too. If you have two offers does one include you speaking at conferences, publishing, or blogging?

- Location. Is there a city you must work in? Are you open to moving? Here in the Bay Area it's common for people to move to San Francisco because it's a city they've always wanted to live in. It's also common for some people to leave later in their career for cost of living reasons. They move away so they can buy a house at half the price. Are you focusing on job offers in specific locations because your spouse has a job there or to be closer to family?

- Commute. I've coached people who were on the verge of leaving a dream job solely because they had a commute from hell. This is a serious factor for many people because a horrible commute affects our quality of life. Will one job offer let you work from home one or two days a week? Are you able to take a bus or train with Wi-Fi to work?

- Work / life balance. Are you about to join a nine to fiver? An eight to sixer? A startup where you're expected to work seventy or more hours a week? Will you be expected to respond to email evenings and weekends? How much vacation will you get?

- Family-friendly. Does your possible company provide or support daycare? One thing I loved about my last company was that some employees would occasionally bring their kids to work and it was entirely welcomed. If a parent leaves work early for their child's class play or sports game is that supported or will it be viewed negatively?

- Are there other decision factors I haven't named that are on your list? If so, include them in your ranking.

After you rank your Top 5 factors compare your two offers. Which of them gives you most or all of the factors critical to you? Also, ask yourself if you have a non-negotiable trump factor. I've coached people where they actually had certain criteria that had to be met for them to even consider the company. For some people that means a certain maximum travel, minimum vacation, maximum commute, etc. If the company wouldn't meet their criteria they'd cross them off their list even if it were an excellent opportunity in numerous other ways.

The other exercise I recommend is to do a Strengths, Weaknesses, Opportunities, and Threat (SWOT) analysis. Typically, strengths and weaknesses are internal looking. Meaning, in one column list all the strengths and weaknesses, pros and cons, of taking both offers. Perhaps the pros for taking the offer from company A are job role and responsibility, your boss, and company culture. The cons for company A might be lower total compensation, shorter vacation, and longer commute. The opportunities and threats are external looking. Perhaps the opportunities for company A are that they are the industry leader and they are in a rapidly growing industry. The threats for company A, if it's a pharmaceutical company, might be that the patent for their best-selling drug is running out and three generics are about to start competing against it, and changing regulations are expected to impede growth unless they change strategy. Do a SWOT analysis for every offer you have and see which opportunity is greater.

By reviewing Step Two to determine your best ecosystem, ranking your Top 5 decision factors, and doing a SWOT analysis you should be able to decide which opportunity to take. Once you make your choice, this chapter of your life is over and the new chapter in your new job is about to begin. If you're still having trouble choosing between offers even after doing these exercises, follow your heart.

Summary

Chapter 18: Having to choose between multiple opportunities is a "problem" most people would love to have.

- To choose between two opportunities start by evaluating which job offer will best enable you to optimize your personal ecosystem.
- Rank the Top 5 factors that are most important to you and compare your two offers. Which of them gives you most or all of the factors critical to you?
- Ask yourself if you have a non-negotiable factor that trumps all other factors.
- Do a Strengths, Weaknesses, Opportunities, and Threat (SWOT) analysis for every offer you have and see which opportunity is stronger.
- If you're still having trouble choosing between offers even after doing these exercises, follow your heart.

Conclusion: *You Got the Job!*

After you get the job you'll want to update your mindset. You're no longer going to be focused like a laser on getting hired. Now you need to shift your focus to getting off to the fastest start possible in your new company by achieving quick wins. But don't make the mistake others make after getting hired, which is to shut down their momentum in creating new connections. Strengthen your relationships with your career agents by taking them to lunch and sending them referrals whenever possible. Remember, a recruiter may be the reason you got your job. That's someone you want to build a long-term partnership with. Keep your resume and Linkedin profile up to date. Perhaps most importantly, always continue to learn. Identify and then acquire the skills you need in both your new job and for the next steps on your career path. If there's one asset you can't keep up to date, let it be your resume because you can update that quickly. But don't let your skill acquisition lapse because certain skills take months or longer to build.

And after you get hired, I want to ask you to do one more exercise. Draw up a list of everyone who helped you get hired and then express your gratitude to them. Your list might include a former colleague who connected you to a recruiter, a recruiter who introduced you to a hiring manager, a colleague at your new company, who, after they interviewed you, gave you advice on what to emphasize during your interview with the hiring manager, a friend who helped you prepare for your interviews, a former boss who provided a glowing recommendation for you, and a loved one who supported you every step of the way and never doubted you even if in moments you doubted yourself.

Moving forward you will have opportunities to help people during their job search. Please do so. Just as you were helped by people during your search, now is the time to pay it back and help others so they can get hired, too. I can tell you from the people we coach during a job search the most gratifying moment for them is being able to say, “I got the job!” But another gratifying experience is being able to help someone else get hired so they can celebrate the same success.

Here’s wishing you success and fulfillment in your new job.

Your company is lucky to have you.

Printed in Great Britain
by Amazon

46189867R00106